P-51 MUSTANG
COMBAT MISSIONS

P-51 MUSTANG

COMBAT MISSIONS

FIRST-HAND ACCOUNTS OF P-51 MUSTANG OPS OVER NAZI EUROPE

MARTIN BOWMAN

METRO BOOKS

NEW YORK

METRO BOOKS
New York
An Imprint of Sterling Publishing
387 Park Avenue South
New York, NY 10016

Editorial Director: **Will Steeds**
Project Editor: **Chris McNab**
Designer: **Philip Clucas** MCSD
Photographers: **Martin Bowman/Mark Winwood/Patrick Bunce**
Production: **Alastair Gourlay**
Color reproduction: **Pixel Colour Imaging, London, England**

Jacket and front cover illustration: *What a Doll!* by Roy Grinnell.

ISBN: 978-1-4351-4612-9

For information about custom editions, special sales, and premium and corporate purchases, please
contact Sterling Special Sales at 800-805-5489 or specialsales@sterlingpublishing.com

Manufactured in China

10 9 8 7 6 5 4 3 2

www.sterlingpublishing.com

Roy Grinnell, Official Artist of the American Fighter Aces Association and the American Combat Airman Hall of Fame
(Commemorative Air Force) was an honors graduate of the Art Center School in Los Angeles. He has received many honors
and awards including the R.G. Smith Award for Excellence in Naval Aviation Art, becoming an Honorary Ace of the AFAA,
and most recently the opening of the Roy Grinnell Gallery in the American Airpower Heritage Museum (CAF) in Midland, TX.
He is also well known for his Western and Native American art. Grinnell's oil paintings have been displayed throughout the
world in museums and private collections. His work also features on the covers of *B-24 Combat Missions*, *B-29 Combat
Missions* and *Spitfire: Life of the Legend* (website: www.roygrinnell.com).

Contents

Introduction

After the war General Henry H. "Hap" Arnold frankly admitted that it had been "the USAAF's own fault" that the North American P-51 Mustang had not been employed operationally very much earlier. Inexplicably, US Army Air Forces (USAAF) planners had considered the Mustang more suitable as a tactical aircraft than as a long-range escort fighter and, in November 1943, the first deliveries of P-51Bs to England were made to three fighter groups in the tactical 9th Air Force at the expense of the strategic 8th Fighter Command.

Ken Blakebrough, a B-17 pilot in the 457th Bomb Group, spoke for all the bomber crews when he said, "The American concept of daylight bombing by bombers, which could protect themselves, was ridiculous. The P-51 saved our necks." General Ira Eaker, commanding 8th Bomber Command, knew that deep-penetration missions were finished unless a proven long-range escort fighter could be found. "At this point nothing was more critical than the early arrival of the P-38s and P-51s," he said, although he saw the Mustang as a tactical and ground-support fighter.

When the 357th Fighter Group, equipped with P-51B Mustangs, arrived at Raydon, Essex, in England it was assigned to the 9th Air Force. Lockheed's P-38 Lightning was not the total solution for long-range fighter escort duties. That would only come with the introduction of the P-51B Mustang, but when this magnificent fighter finally entered combat, on December 1, 1943, it was as a tactical fighter with the 354th Fighter Group, 9th Air Force, flying a sweep over Belgium. The first Mustang fighter-escort mission for the bombers was not flown until December 5, 1943. On December 11, using drop tanks, the Mustangs ranged as far as Emden to support B-17s bombing the German port.

On December 13, in a record-setting mission, when 649 bombers attacked the port areas of Bremen and Hamburg, and the U-boat yards at Kiel, P-51s reached the limit of their escort range for the first time. This was also the first occasion on which more than 600 American bombers had attacked targets in a single day.

Lieutenant Colonel Don Blakeslee, CO of the 4th Fighter Group but assigned to the 354th Fighter Group to help them enter combat, was so impressed with the P-51B that when he returned to his unit at Debden he argued forcefully to be equipped with the Mustang. Blakeslee pleaded with his general to exchange their old Thunderbolts for them. However, a great daylight offensive was planned and the Normandy invasion would take place within three months, so the general answered that he did not see how Blakeslee's group could become non-operational for several weeks while they re-trained on the new fighter. "That's OK, General, sir," replied Don. "We can learn to fly them on the way to the target!" Blakeslee got his P-51s at the end of February 1944. His total victory score was 14.5, seven of which were scored flying P-51B/D aircraft.

It was not until the 357th Fighter Group and its P-51Bs was transferred to the 8th Air Force in December 1943 in exchange for the P-47 Thunderbolt-equipped 358th Fighter Group that the 8th had its own long-range escort fighter. The P-51s flew their first escort mission on February 11, 1944. In March that year P-51Bs would fly to Berlin and back for the first time.

The Mustang was the straw that would eventually break the back of the *Jagdgruppen* (in particular, the twin-engined fighters of the *Zerstörergruppen* were no match for the P-51). The P-51B was not only capable of meeting Bf 109s and Fw 190s on even or better terms; it could escort the B-24s and B-17s to their targets and back again. The Mustang's range of 2,080 miles (3,347km), achieved by the use of wing drop tanks, was far in excess of that provided by other fighters of the day.

Hermann Göring, the Luftwaffe fighter chief, is said to have remarked, "We have lost the war!" when he finally believed the reporting center of the appearance over Hanover of the Mustang. The P-51's advantage of greater endurance than the P-47 Thunderbolt saw it regularly running up substantial scores as the Mustang entered widespread use as an escort fighter on long-penetration raids deep into Germany.

In 1944, 14 P-51 groups and one P-47 group were serving in the 8th Air Force; at the same time 14 P-47 groups, three P-51 groups, and one P-38 fighter group were serving in the 9th Air Force. By the end of the war, the P-51 equipped all but one of the 8th Air Force fighter groups. Elsewhere the Mustang's extreme range made it a natural choice for bomber-escort and fighter sweeps in the Pacific, and the 5th Air Force in the Pacific Theater of Operations received P-51Ds to equip three groups to support B-29 attacks against Japan. The RAF operated 16 Merlin-powered Mustang squadrons in the UK and six in Italy at the war's end. Other users included China and Australia.

Altogether, 15,484 examples of this remarkable aircraft were built with 5,541 of these aircraft in frontline service with the USAAF at war's end. From 1942 to 1945, Mustangs flew 213,873 sorties, with 2,520 aircraft being lost in combat. Mustang pilots claimed 4,950 enemy aircraft destroyed in the air (compared to 3,082 by the P-47) and another 4,131 on the ground (compared to 3,202 by the P-47). The P-51's record represented a loss rate of 1.2 percent per sortie, compared to 0.7 percent for the P-47, which in total suffered losses of 3,077 aircraft in 423,435 sorties.

Today, enthusiasm for the Mustang remains undiminished and examples refurbished by Florida's Cavalier Aircraft in the late 1960s and even derelict P-51s are acquired for rebuild to flying condition for the "warbird" air show circuit. All have ensured that the aircraft is actually increasing in numbers on the aircraft registers of the world. At the time of writing there are 297 surviving Mustangs, of which 154 are airworthy, 53 are being restored, and 24 are in store. Today, the Mustang is a living legend and is remembered as probably the finest long-range single-seat piston-engined fighter ever built.

Martin W. Bowman

Norwich, England

PART 1
History & Development

History and Development

"The P-51B felt slightly heavier than the A and you could sense the difference in the engines—the Allison slower and lower in pitch, the Packard somewhat more chattery and permitting higher manifold pressure. But once past 20,000ft [6,096m], with the high blower in, the B really came alive. It sped upward with an excellent rate of climb, to about an indicated 43,000ft [13,107m], a new part of the world for most fighter pilots. This was truly the very best fighter that the USAAF had. What an engine! It was still fast, like the P-51A at low altitudes and it had even greater range, which we Aleutian pilots could appreciate."

—Colonel (later Major General) Charles M. "Sandy" McCorkle, an ace on both Mustangs and Spitfires in Italy, 1943–44, who flew the P-51B in Florida after his unit had been recalled from combat duty with P-39s in the Aleutians

During the 1930s North American Aviation (NAA) of Inglewood, California in the Los Angeles area built aircraft that included the all-metal O-47 observation plane and the equally innovative BT-9 basic trainer. The company also produced the BC-l, which substituted a retractable landing gear for the BT-9's fixed undercarriage. In summer 1938, the British Purchasing Commission placed orders for 200 of these, which, with modifications to Royal Air Force (RAF) requirements, became the Harvard, or AT-6/SNJ Texan in US service. NAA then entered the bomber business with the twin-engined NA-40 attack bomber, which later developed into the B-25 Mitchell medium bomber. In July 1938 came the experimental NA-44 light attack bomber.

In February 1940, North American first considered the NA-73 fighter project that later developed into the Mustang. Representatives of the British Air Ministry had asked the company to build Curtiss P-40 fighters but, after considering this proposal, the company suggested that it be

Above: *"Dutch" Kindleberger and John Atwood, President and Vice President of North American Aviation.*

permitted to build a new type of its own design, incorporating all the latest aerodynamic refinements and all knowledge gained in air combat since the outbreak of the war. This proposal was accepted by the British Purchasing Commission late in the spring of 1940 and design drafting on the new fighter began on May 5.

A team was assembled, headed up by H. C. B. Thomas of the British Purchasing Commission and North American President, J. H. "Dutch" Kindleberger, with Ray H. Rice (Vice President Engineering), German-born Edgar Schmued, (Chief Designer), who had previously worked for Fokker and Messerschmitt, J. S. Smithson (Manufacturing) and a few others. They sat down in Washington, DC over a weekend and came up with a specification for the NA-73, plus cost estimates. The British approved the contract and Allison agreed to increase the production of the V-1710 engine. Completion of the first airplane (less engine) on September 9, 1940, just 127 days after design drafting started, dramatically pointed to

Below: *First XP-51 (41-038) on an early test flight. The NA-73X was of all-metal stressed skin construction. The wings, which had pronounced dihedral, contained a sheet-web main spar and an almost equally strong rear spar, which carried the ailerons and flaps.*

Above: *Engineers carry out a static test on NA-73X at Inglewood, California to test the wing-to-fuselage structural joint.*

Right: *The Mustang I AG633 XV-E on 2 Squadron RAF, seen here in July 1942.*

one of the greatest aeronautical engineering feats of the war.

In 1938 "Dutch" Kindelberger had visited Germany and he had toured the Heinkel and Messerschmitt plants. He liked what he saw and he adopted a radiator air scoop for the design, placed ventrally and as far aft as possible. This kept it away from fin and fuselage drag. It incorporated entrance and exit ducts, which reduced the drag of the air-scoop dramatically. This reduction created a ramjet effect that enhanced performance. Dr Shenstone of the British Air Ministry further increased efficiency by providing an upper lip on the radiator housing 1½ inches (38mm) below the fuselage's contour and this, when combined with a small gap between the lip and the fuselage, reduced turbulence and therefore drag, even further. The Mustang's low drag was largely due to the characteristics of the wing airfoil section (which represented the first practical application of the National Advisory Committee For Aeronautics (NACA) laminar flow theory), the efficiency of the cooling system, and the cleanness of contour and low frontal area of the fuselage.

Although many compromises were made in the Mustang design, the company did have the advantage of starting with a clean slate without an insurmountable handicap of existing arrangements, limiting production practices and rutted design thinking. The first test flight of the experimental Mustang was made on October 26, 1940, from Mines Field (today Los Angeles International Airport) adjoining the factory in Inglewood.

More than 2,800 original drawings were made during the design process, which enabled the experimental shop to build a $20,000 quarter-sized mahogany model, built to 0.001-inch tolerances, which underwent critical wind tunnel testing. Full-scale drawings enabled patterns (templates) to be made for production use. The powerplant was the 12-cylinder Allison V-1710-39 V-12 liquid-cooled, inline engine, with a single-speed, single-stage supercharger. It developed 1,120hp at 3,000rpm.

foreign combatants could obtain much-needed aircraft from American sources, in effect, paying for the tooling-up and expansion of the rapidly growing US military aviation base prior to their involvement in the war.

To ensure strict legality under the neutrality laws the first production Mustangs were designated as the P-51-NA and they had to be purchased for use by the USAAF first and then Lend-Leased to Britain as the Mustang Mk I. They mounted four 20mm cannon as their armament. On May 29, 1941, 320 NA-73s were ordered. A further order was placed for 300 slightly improved NA-82 aircraft, the order being completed in July 1942. First production deliveries were made in the fall of 1941 and the

Below: P-51Ds on the production line at Dallas with T-6 trainers in Soviet Air Force markings.

Above left and above right: *Here we see Mustangs on the production line at Inglewood, California. Note the gun hatches open in the wings. In the image to the right, a shipping department employee at the North American Aviation plant drills holes in a shipment.*

Test pilot Vance Breese flew the NA-73X on its October 26 first flight and forty-five flights had been conducted with two prototypes by July 15, 1941. However, the initial prototype crashed on its ninth flight, when test pilot Paul Balfour, after making two high-speed runs over Mines Field on November 20, 1940, omitted to put the fuel valve on "reserve" while making a third run. As a result the engine, starved of fuel, suddenly cut out and Balfour attempted to make a hasty wheels-down landing on a newly plowed farm field. The Mustang's wheels dug themselves into the mud, flipping the aircraft onto its back. Although Balfour was unhurt, the aircraft itself was a total write-off and the test program had to be completed with a second prototype.

Even before the XP-51 had completed its flight testing program at Wright Field, 150 P-51 fighters were ordered on July 7, 1941, by the USAAF on behalf of the RAF. Under the Lend-Lease program that President Franklin D. Roosevelt pushed through a reluctant Congress,

Mustang entered operational service with the Royal Air Force in November 1941. At least 20 Mustang Is were lost at sea and another ten were diverted to the Soviet Union before the end of 1941 and which were used against Finland.

A Lend-Lease contract approved on September 25, 1941, added 150 NA-91s to the production schedule. These differed from the initial production aircraft by having self-sealing fuel tanks and four 20mm cannon replacing the armament of eight machine-guns. Glowing reports from the American test pilots who had flown the two XP-51 prototypes meanwhile, aroused Air Corps interest and Major General O. P. Echols,

Channel by the 107th TRS on December 20, 1943. Another two P-51-1-NA aircraft were kept in the United States to undertake experimental trials with the licence-built Rolls-Royce Merlin engine (XP-78) under development by the Packard Company of Detroit. Testing by the USAAF of its XP-51 prototypes had confirmed RAF findings of the deficiency in high-altitude performance, a weakness explored in the UK by the experimental installation of Rolls-Royce Merlin 61 and 65 engines. The Packard Merlin was a better engine than that produced by Rolls-Royce due to superior production methods and some minor redesign that was approved by Rolls-Royce.

On May 29, 1942, the first P-51 made its maiden flight piloted by Louis Watt. Despite its strong performance at lower altitudes, the Mustang IA was handicapped at high altitudes by the Allison engine's lack of power and so it was decided to operate the Mustang on armed tactical reconnaissance sorties instead of in the fighter role. Mustangs began equipping No. 22 RAF Army Co-operation Squadron in April 1942. The aircraft made its operational debut on May 5, 1942, when a Mustang I of No. 26 Squadron at Gatwick flew a 1-hour 40-minute tactical reconnaissance sortie of part of the French coast, during which hangars at Berck airfield and a train near La Fesnesie were strafed. By May six squadrons were working up on the new fighter. Following the disbandment of Army Co-Operation Command in June 1943, the

Above: A 2nd TAF Mustang Mark I on 168 Squadron RAF caught on camera on August 14, 1944, during a steep turn.

Right: Test Pilot Paul Balfour attempted a wheels-down landing when the engine of NA-73X stopped while flying at 250ft (76m) over Mines Field (now Los Angeles Airport) on November 20, 1940.

Assistant Chief of Air Staff, responsible for Material, Maintenance and Distribution, had begun pressing for an American version of this aircraft.

As a result, the RAF received only ninety-three NA-91s (Mustang IA), while fifty-five were retained by the USAAC as the P-51-1-NA and were later converted to photographic reconnaissance aircraft with the designation P-51-2-NA (later F-6A), with two cameras behind the cockpit for tactical reconnaissance duties. They were sent to the 68th Observation Group, whose 154th Squadron flew the first AAF photo recon mission on April 9, 1943. Also in 1943 35 P-51A-10s were converted to F-6B standard and they were first sent out across the English

Mustang squadrons temporarily joined RAF Fighter Command before being absorbed into the new 2nd Tactical Air Force. Around 600 Mustang IIIs and IVs (282 P-51Ds and about 400 P-51Ks) equipped sixteen squadrons of the RAF in the UK and the 2nd Tactical Air Force in Europe, and six squadrons in the Mediterranean at the war's end. Of the many Mustangs that entered service with the RAF, some were still serving with Fighter Command as late as November 1946.

In America, meanwhile, the Defense Budget for the Fiscal Year 1942 had already been spent for purchase of aircraft in the "Pursuit" category but the US Army Air Corps (USAAC) exploited the "Attack" aircraft budget, which was still in surplus. Lieutenant General Henry H. "Hap" Arnold, chief of the Air Corps, saw the merits of the dive-bomber following the continued successes of the German Junkers Ju 87 Stuka in Europe and the Mediterranean.

Hydraulically operated lattice type dive-brakes used on the Vultee Vengeance which opened both above and below each wing, were applied to the Mustang. A pair of under-wing bomb shackles, capable of toting a single 500lb bomb apiece, was installed outboard of the undercarriage. Designated A-36 Apache, the dive-bomber Mustang entered the USAAF inventory in North Africa, where the pilots soon recognized it as a far better fighter airplane than the P-40 or P-38. Meanwhile, in the fall of 1942, Lieutenant Colonel Thomas Hitchcock (later killed flying a

Above: *Wooden wheels were attached to the Mustang on the production lines at Inglewood, California, so that aircraft could be moved around the ramp.*

Left: *A war-weary P-51B is overhauled at the 8th Air Force's repair and replacement center at the 3rd Base Air Depot (3 BAD) at Warton in Lancashire, 1944.*

Mustang), the US military attaché in London, suggested to Washington at the encouragement of Ambassador J. G. Winant that the Mustang be developed as a long-range fighter fitted with the Rolls-Royce Merlin engine. Hitchcock reported that the P-51 was one of the best, if not *the* best fighter airframes developed and advised its development as a high-altitude fighter by mating it with the Merlin 61 engine. This engine, with its two-stage, two-speed supercharger in place of the single-stage unit in the earlier Merlin XX, promised a top speed of 400mph (644kmph) at 30,000ft (9,144m).

An early concept, tried in mock-up form, was to position the engine behind the pilot with an extension shaft driving the propeller rather like the Allison-powered Bell P-39 Airacobra. This idea, however, was rejected and the Merlin was mounted in the conventional position in the nose with the intercooler radiator beneath it. Eddie Rickenbacker endorsed the concept of fitting the Merlin to the P-51 and four Mustang Is were

delivered to Rolls-Royce at Hucknall, near Derby, for conversion to Mustang Xs, with the first in the air by October 13, 1942. Data on this work was sent to the United States and North American was issued a contract on July 31, 1942, for two XP-78 to be converted from Lend-Lease P-51s. The XP-78 designation changed in September 1942 to XP-51B (NA-101). The aircraft were to be fitted with the V-1650-3 Merlin licence-built by the Packard Motor Company. With its two-stage supercharger the engine was rated by the Air Force at 1,295hp at 28,750ft (8,763m), with a 1,595hp war emergency rating available to 17,000ft (5,181m). The first Packard Merlin Mustang flew on November 30, 1942, fitted with a four-bladed Hamilton propeller to give it better high-altitude performance than the three-bladed propeller of earlier models, and the up-draught carburettor intake below, instead of above, the engine. The intercooler was incorporated in a redesigned main radiator assembly in the existing ventral position amidships and new

The last 350 P-51B-15-NAs were powered by the V-1650-7 (Merlin 68), which had a war emergency rating of 1,695hp at 10,300ft (3,139m) and produced a maximum speed of 439mph (706kmph) at 25,000ft (7,620m). In August 1943 a new factory at Dallas, Texas, began deliveries of 350 P-51C-1-NT Mustangs powered by the V-1650-3, followed by 1,400 P-51Cs powered by the V-1650-7. The P-51C had increased internal fuel capacity and a British-designed Malcolm bulged frameless sliding hood similar to the Spitfire canopy as a temporary measure to improve the rearward view. R. Malcolm's design was fitted to most RAF Mustang IIIs, as well as to a number of USAAF P-51Bs and F-6s.

Left: An early P-51B. This aircraft later served in the UK. The cockpit was roomy by British standards, with 0.31in (8mm) back armor to protect the pilot.

Below: P-51Ds of the 458th Fighter Squadron, 506th Fighter Group, assemble for take off from the runway at North Field for another escort mission to Japan.

ailerons were fitted. The XP-51B aircraft demonstrated a maximum speed of 441mph (709kmph) at 29,800ft (9,083m) and the XP-51B configuration was selected to replace the P-51A.

The first production P-51B-1-NA powered by the Packard-built V-1650-3 Merlin was flown on May 5, 1943, and North American's Inglewood factory went on to produce 1,788 P-51Bs (NA-102 and NA-104). The P-51B differed from the earlier versions by having a strengthened fuselage and redesigned ailerons. When another fuel tank was added behind the cockpit, and with two 108- or 150-gallon (409- or 564-liter) drop tanks below the wings, the Mustang had the range needed to accompany bombers to any target in Germany.

Armament was still four .50-caliber guns—half that of a P-47—and gun stoppages due to a combination of factors were commonplace. The laminar wing section was too thin to accommodate the .50-caliber machine guns in the normal upright position so they were canted at about 30°. Thus, the ammunition feed trays had to curve upward slightly and then down again to enable link-belted rounds to enter the gun at the right angle. Gun jams were almost inevitable if they were fired while the pilot was pulling about four Gs. Worse still, all four guns could stop firing altogether.

In 1943 71 Merlin-powered P-51B-ls and 20 P-51C-ls received by the USAAF were modified as F-6C tactical reconnaissance aircraft, their number augmented by F-6D and F-6K conversions of later versions. All of these aircraft still carried their wing guns and frequently used them; the last German fighter destroyed in the war was an Fw 190, downed by an F-6C on May 8, 1945.

The P-51D, which replaced the B model at Inglewood in March 1944, was to become the most successful variant of all Mustangs. It was built in greater quantity than any other variant with a total of 7,956 built; 6,502 at Inglewood and 1,454 at Dallas. From this total 136 were modified as tactical reconnaissance F-6D aircraft and 282 were allocated to the RAF, which designated them Mustang IV. The P-51D differed from earlier versions in having a streamlined "bubble" (teardrop) canopy with a

TP-51D two-seat trainers. The latter had re-located radio equipment to make room for an additional seat, with full dual controls, behind the pilot's seat. One TP-51D was further modified for use as a high-speed observation post for the Supreme Allied Commander, General Eisenhower, who flew in it to inspect the Normandy beachheads in June 1944. Ten 5-inch rockets, two 500lb bombs, or drop tanks could be carried below the wings.

lowered rear decking to give the pilot all-round vision. The new teardrop hood was introduced onto the production line after the completion of the first four aircraft.

Later, a small dorsal fin fairing was added to most P-51D examples to compensate for the loss of keel surface on the rear fuselage. Tail warning radar was also added. Armament was increased to six .50-caliber wing guns with 1,880 rounds. Power was provided by the more powerful Packard Merlin V-1650-7 engine driving a Hamilton propeller. This was the fastest of all Mustangs, having a top speed of 487mph (783kmph). With external tanks giving a total of 489 US gallons (1,851 liters) of fuel, the P-51D was comparatively light at 11,600lb (5,272kg) and had an absolute range of 2,080 miles (3,347km) and an endurance of 8½ hours.

As well as P-51Ds the Texas factory also produced 1,337 P-51Ks (similar except for an Aeroproducts four-bladed, clipped-tip propeller that was introduced following the reported shortage of the Hamilton Standard propeller), 163 F-6K tactical reconnaissance variants and ten

Above left: A-36As being serviced at a base in the southeast United States.

Above right: P-51B Mustang 43-24853/U in the 52nd Fighter Group, 15th Air Force, which overshot the runway and landed in a pond.

Left: The St. Louis Star Times headlines announce the American declaration of war after the Japanese bombing of Pearl Harbor. Germany declared war on the United States the following day.

A new lightweight fighter design (NA-105) purely for air-to-air combat was offered in January 1943, with no provision for bombing or ground attack. A July 20 contract called for five prototypes. The first NA-105, an XP-51F with Packard V-1650-3 (later V-1650-7), flew on February 14, 1944 while the fourth, an XP-51G, flew on August 9 with an imported Rolls-Royce Merlin 145 and a unique five-bladed propeller. The third XP-51F was sent to England on June 30, 1944 for evaluation at Boscombe Down as the Mustang V, and the second XP-51G also went to Britain on February 1, 1945, and was designated Mustang VI.

Two more prototypes were ordered in June, designated XP-51J. The first was flown on April 23, 1945, with an Allison V-1710-119 with water injection. Both the XP-51F and the XP-51G revealed heavy rudder forces and a lack of directional stability in some flight attitudes. A number of notable modifications had to be made before the P-51H, a refined XP-51F, could become the first lightweight Mustang to enter production. The P-51H differed from the P-51F in having an upgraded Packard V-1650-9 engine fitted with water injection and automatic boost control (the Merlin 100 series was not yet in full production) and driving a four-bladed Aeroproducts propeller. Other new features included a P-51D-type canopy and increased internal fuel capacity.

A thousand P-51Hs were ordered on June 30, 1944, from Inglewood with the first P-51H-1-NA flying on February 3, 1945. The P-51H was probably the fastest propeller-driven aircraft actually produced in wartime. Top speed was 487mph (784kmph) at 25,000ft (7,620m) when used as an interceptor, or 450mph (724kmph) when carrying two 500lb bombs and added fuel. Range with two 110-gallon (416-liter) drop tanks could be extended to 2,400 miles (3,862km) at 241mph (388kmph) or 850 miles (1,367km) when carrying two 1,000lb bombs. Armament was six .50-caliber guns, plus optional external loads comprising the two bombs or ten 5-inch rockets. Ammunition supply included 400 rounds for each inner-wing gun and 270 rounds for each of the others. Armor included $\frac{7}{16}$-inch (11mm) plate behind the pilot's head, $\frac{5}{16}$-inch (8mm) behind his back, and ¼-inch at the front fire wall.

Only 555 P-51Hs had been built when the war's end brought cancellation of the balance of 2,000 ordered, the last being completed on November 9, 1945. Also cancelled were 1,700 similar V-1650-11 powered P-51L and 1,628 P-51M fighters, which were to be the Dallas-built version of the P-51H. Only a single example (the last P-51D-30-NT) was actually completed and flown in August 1945 as a P-51M with a 1,400hp Packard V-1650-9A.

Forty P-51Ds and ten P-51Ks were Lend-Leased to two Dutch East Indies squadrons but they were too late to enter combat against Japan. China had received P-51C Mustangs to replace the P-40s of the Chinese-American Composite Wing and with the arrival of P-51Ds in 1945 three Chinese groups were equipped with Mustangs. New Zealand purchased 30 P-51D-25-NTs in 1945 and that same year Australia replaced its P-40s with 84 P-51K and 214 P-51D Mustangs from Texas, along with imported components for the first 80 Mustang Mk 20s that were assembled by Commonwealth Aircraft Corporation. The first was flown on April 29, 1945.

Mustang production ended in the United States on the grand total of 15,386, flying 213,800 combat sorties in USAAF service during World War II. Licence construction by Commonwealth Aircraft followed for the Royal Australian Air Force (RAAF) with 26 Mustang Mk 21 aircraft

Bore-Sighting Diagram

This Bore-Sighting Diagram appeared in the North American P-51 manual to show how the guns were to be configured for aiming. Fighter machine guns did not fire in parallel, but instead all aimed towards a "point of convergence" at a set distance in front of the aircraft. This point of fire was configured on the ground at a fixed target, with the guns being sighted down the bore.

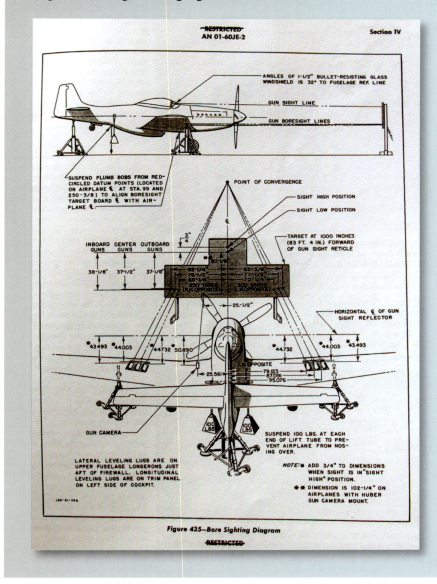

Figure 435—Bore Sighting Diagram

powered by V-1650-7 engines. Fourteen were later converted to Mustang Mk 22s, and they were followed by 67 Mustang Mk 23 aircraft with Merlin 66 or 70 engines and 13 Mustang Mk 22s for tactical reconnaissance; none of these RAAF aircraft saw service before VJ-Day.

Combat History

The Mustang will forever be identified with its exploits in the ETO—the European Theater of Operations. During "Big Week" (February 20–25, 1944) 8th and 15th Air Force bombers and 1,000 fighters were dispatched almost daily on the deepest penetrations into Germany thus far. In the first week of March 1944, P-51Bs flew to Berlin and back for the first time. On March 6, 801 P-38s, P-47s and P-51s of the 4th, 354th and 357th Fighter Groups escorted 730 B-17s and B-24s to targets in the suburbs of "Big-B," as Berlin was known. Eleven fighters, five of them Mustangs, were lost but the P-51s claimed forty-one enemy aircraft destroyed.

On March 8 the 4th Fighter Group claimed 16 enemy aircraft destroyed on another mission to Berlin. During March the 4th Fighter Group also claimed no fewer than 156 confirmed air-to-air victories plus eight "probables," and 100 more were claimed in just 15 days. On April 5 Mustangs took part in the first large-scale USAAF all-fighter sweep, to the Berlin and Munich areas. It involved a round trip of 1,200 miles (1,931km).

These long missions signalled the beginning of the end of Luftwaffe air superiority over the Reich. The Mustang's advantage of greater endurance than the P-47 saw it regularly running up substantial scores as the P-51 saw widespread use as an escort fighter on long-penetration raids deep into Germany. By 1945, 14 P-51 groups and one P-47 group served the 8th Air Force, while 14 P-47 groups, three P-51 groups, and one P-38 fighter group served the 9th Air Force. The top Mustang group was the 357th, with 609 air and 106 ground kills from February 11, 1944 to April 25, 1945. The 4th Group, which used Spitfires, P-47s, and P-51s (received in February 1944), had 583 air and 469 ground kills.

The RAF was second only to the USAAF in Mustang operation. Lend-Lease allocations of the P-51B/C versions for the RAF comprised 308 and 636, respectively, all designated Mustang III, but some were repossessed

Above: A crew chief of the 332nd Fighter Group examines some superficial skin damage to the tail of his P-51C Mustang. The damage was caused by an exploding anti-aircraft shell

by the USAAF. The first unit to be equipped was 65 Squadron, which received its first Mustang III in December 1943, but the type did not enter service with the RAF until February 1944 when it began equipping 19 Squadron at Ford. The first 250 ordered had the older, hinged cockpit canopy. With a maximum speed of 442mph (711kmph) at 24,500ft (7,468m), it was more than a match for German propeller-driven fighters in 1944 and could operate far over the continent with the aid of drop tanks.

From the spring of 1944, the Mustang III served with the Desert Air Force supporting the 8th Army in Italy and was flown by 239 Wing in eastern Italy, comprising the RAF's 112 and 260 Squadrons, RAAF's 3 Squadron and the South African 5 Squadron. The latter changed over to Mustangs from Curtiss P-40 Kittyhawks. On May 5, soon after the first unit (260 Squadron) had received Mustangs, both types of aircraft from the wing destroyed the great Pescara Dam by bombing. Not one Mustang was lost on this operation, which was a remarkable feat to be accomplished by single-seat fighters.

No. 239 Wing's Mustangs were responsible for evolving the "cab-rank" tactics that were subsequently used to equally good effect in northern Europe. The Mustangs, sometimes carrying bombs, patrolled above the forward troops during an offensive, usually in a line astern formation. The Mustangs awaited radio calls from a mobile observation post embedded with the troops for attacks on specific targets previously located by spotter aircraft. On receiving a call one or more aircraft from the "cab-rank" would dive upon the target and drop bombs or strafe it with gunfire. Both the ground controllers and the Mustang pilots used the same photographic map with a grid superimposed upon it and "Rover David"—as the system was code-named—proved an immediate success. Various modifications of the system were tried from time to time as the war continued, but its principle remained unchanged.

Mustang IIIs continued to escort medium and heavy bombers over the continent in 1944 and after the Normandy landings in June 1944 some Mustang squadrons in the 2nd Tactical Air Force (TAF) moved to the Continent to act as fighter-bombers. Mustangs operated on everything from offensive sweeps, escorts to Bristol Beaufighters as far afield as Denmark, anti-Diver (V-1 flying bomb) patrols (in a three-month period ending September 5, 1944, Mustangs of 12 Group had destroyed 232 "Doodlebugs"), barge-busting along the River Seine and, from D-Day, giving close air support to Allied troops. Two Mustangs were used by 617 Squadron to mark targets for the heavies of Bomber Command.

By September 1944, two Italian-based Mustang III squadrons—213 and 249 at Biferno in the Balkan Air Force—were busy operating over Yugoslavia and Greece. It was in Italy and the Balkans that rocket-firing Mustangs were first used, following trials at the Aeroplane and Armament

Above: *P-51A of the 530th Fighter Squadron, 311th Fighter Bomber Group undergoes battle damage repairs at Kurmitola in Burma in 1943.*

Left: *P-51Cs of the 51st Fighter Group (often confused with the similarly shark-mouthed 23rd Fighter Group "Flying Tigers") lined up on a Chinese airfield, 1944.*

Experimental Establishment (A&AEE) at Boscombe Down of a Mk V rocket projectile installation on a Mustang III. As the rocket kit greatly reduced the aircraft's speed, it did not find favor for operations in Northern Europe, although they were acceptable in Italy. USAAF Mustangs in various war zones also used rockets, their weapons often being fired from infantry-type bazookas, whereas the RAF Mustangs launched rockets from rails.

All told, Mustang IIIs and IVs equipped eighteen squadrons of the RAF in the UK and 2nd Tactical Air Force (TAF), and six squadrons in the Mediterranean. At the end of 1944 Mustangs of the 2nd TAF were with-

drawn and rejoined Fighter Command but Mustangs of 11 and 13 Groups continued to escort US 8th Air Force daylight raids from the UK until the end of the war.

On March 19, 1945, USAAF Mustangs flew 606 sorties in support of the bombers, and over 100 enemy fighters including 36 jets in formation (the largest number yet seen in one formation) were encountered. US fighters claimed forty-two enemy fighters (including three jets) destroyed. On March 21, 1945, 78th Fighter Group Mustangs claimed five Me 262 jet fighters destroyed, three of which were caught at low level after taking off from their airfield. In Italy four fighter groups (the 31st, 52nd, 325th, and 332nd) replaced older types with P-51s, which joined the 15th Air Force's three P-38 groups for the war's last year in Europe.

The comparative performance of aircraft was an obvious preoccupation for Allied aviation designers. Throughout 1942 the Air Fighting Development Unit (AFDU) at Duxford tested a variety of British and American aircraft. Chief among them was the Mustang. Flight tests showed that the Allison-engined Mustang I could consistently reach a top speed of 375mph (603kmph) at 15,000ft (4,572m), 35mph (56kmph) faster than the Spitfire V. The Mustang was heavier than the Spitfire V—about 8,600lb (3,909kg) loaded as compared to 6,900lb (3,136kg)—and therefore did not climb as quickly, taking 11 minutes to reach 20,000ft (6,096m) as opposed to seven minutes for the Spitfire. Above 15,000ft (4,572m) the performance of the Mustang fell away because of lack of any supercharging

on the Allison engine. A four-hour endurance was almost twice that of the Spitfire or other contemporary single-engined fighters. Its critical altitude was reached at 12,000ft (3,658m), above which performance gradually fell off until at 25,000ft (7,620m) the aircraft became quite unwieldy to control. In comparison tests the Mustang proved faster than the Spitfire VB in level flight up to 20,000ft (6,096m) and it could frequently turn with the Spitfire at the lower altitudes by judiciously using flaps.

Against the German Bf 109E the Mustang also showed superior maneuverability and speed at low altitudes. The Messerschmitt Bf 109G had a much-inferior performance to the Merlin-engined Mustang but it could out-accelerate and out-climb the Merlin Mustang at low altitudes. The Merlin-engined Mustang eventually achieved a top speed of 433mph (697kmph) and could climb to 20,000ft (6,096m) in 6.3 minutes as opposed to 9.1 for the Mustang I. In exhaustive tests with a captured Bf 109G-6 and a late-production Mustang III the RAF's AFDU discovered that the altitude for maximum performance from the 109G's Daimler Benz DB605A engine was 16,000ft (4,877m), but at this height the Mustang was 30mph (48kmph) faster in level flight and its advantage increased to 50mph (80kmph) at 30,000ft (9,144m). The 109 had a slightly better rate of climb up to 20,000ft (6,096m), but thereafter the Mustang gained a slight advantage. There was little to choose between the two aircraft in rate of roll, though in turning maneuvers the Mustang could always out-turn the 109. In a dive the Mustang could draw steadily away from the Me 109G. Firepower of the 109G was much heavier than the Mustang; three 20mm cannon and two 13mm machine guns, but the 109G lacked endurance, with only about 90 minutes under combat conditions. The Bf 109 pilot also had very restricted visibility from the cockpit.

Against the Fw 190A there was little difference in rate of climb and a slight advantage for the Mustang in turns. The Fw 190 was always out-dived by the Mustang but the German fighter had a vastly superior rate of roll. A March 1944 report by the AFDU made brief comparisons between the P-51B-1 and the Fw 190 powered by the BMW 801D. It stated that the latter was almost 50mph (80kmph) slower at all heights, increasing to 70mph (113kmph) above 28,000ft (8,534m) and it was anticipated that the new DB603-engined Fw 190D might be slightly faster below 27,000ft (8,230m) but slower above that height. There appeared to be little to choose in the maximum rate of climb. It was anticipated that the Mustang III would have a better maximum climb than the new Fw 190. The

Left: The commanders of the four 15th Air Force P-51 groups in formation over Italy in 1945. From the top they are: the red-striped 31st Fighter Group; yellow-tailed 52nd, red-tailed 332nd and checker-tailed 325th.

Below: This Mustang suffered damage after a collision with another fighter. Aircraft frequently took off in pairs, but the P-51's nose often prevented pilots from seeing ahead clearly, leading to some inevitable accidents.

Mustang was considerably faster at all heights in a zoom climb and it could always out-dive the Fw 190. When it came to the turning circle the report stated that there was not much to choose, although the Mustang was considered slightly better. In terms of rate of roll not even a Mustang III approached the Fw 190. The report concluded that, "In the attack, a high speed should be maintained or regained in order to regain height initiative. An Fw 190 could not evade by diving alone. In defense a steep turn followed by a full-throttle dive should increase the range before regaining height and course. Dogfighting is not altogether recommended. Do not attempt to climb away without at least 250mph [402kmph] showing initially."

Though the Mustang was certainly more maneuverable than the much heavier Thunderbolt airplane, most "Jug" pilots considered that the P-51 was nowhere near as resilient to flak damage as the P-47. The Thunderbolt was a robust creature that could always be counted on to get its pilot home, and many pilots were naturally reluctant to change. Even German pilots considered the Mustang to be more vulnerable to cannon fire.

Of all the Mustang variants it was the "D" model that was the most successful, and it was built in greater quantity than any other. It excelled in high-altitude escort and combat, being superior in speed and maneuverability to all Luftwaffe piston-engined fighters above 20,000ft (6,096m). The P-47's low-level performance made it better-suited than the Mustang for the ground-attack role, so the majority of Thunderbolts equipped the 9th and 15th TAF in England and Italy, respectively.

In the early months of 1944, US Mustangs began operating in Burma in support of airborne troops attacking Japanese lines of communication 200 miles (320km) behind the Assam–Burma front. These aircraft subsequently moved forward into China. Merlin-powered Mustangs were used against Japan in 1944 by the 23rd, 51st, and 311th Groups in China, while the 5th Air Force received P-51Ds in 1945 for the 3rd Commando, 35th, and 348th Groups. Perhaps the most significant Mustang missions in the Pacific were those flown to support B-29 attacks against Japan in the final weeks of the war. After the capture of Iwo Jima in February 1945, three P-51D/K Fighter Groups moved in to begin escorting the B-29 Superfortresses in their assault on the Japanese mainland. The first two groups in action were the 15th and 21st Fighter Groups, which after supporting the invasion forces in the area flew their first mission to Japan on April 7, when they escorted B-29s of 20th Bomber Command attacking the heavily-defended Nakajima aircraft factory near Tokyo. This involved a round-trip of almost 1,500 miles (2,414km) and the Mustangs claimed 21 enemy fighters destroyed for the loss of just two fighters, a feat that earned both groups a Distinguished Unit Citation. Thereafter the 15th and 21st—and the 506th from May onwards—continued to fly offensive sweeps and long-range escort missions to Japanese targets until the end of the war.

Although the P-51 had shown exceptional range in Europe, even greater range capability was required in the Pacific theater and this had led, in January 1944, to development of the XP-82 Twin Mustang prototype, the last propeller-driven fighter purchased by the USAAF. The P-82 was, essentially, two P-51H fuselages with one port and one starboard wing eliminated, joined together on a single parallel-chord wing

Above: P-51 42-103 "Big Mamma" in the 11th Tactical Reconnaissance Squadron in the 12th Air Force. Italy was originally selected for USAAF operations due to its proximity to targets out of range of the 8th Air Force.

section and stabilizer and a new tailplane and elevator. The revised main landing gear comprised a retractable main wheel underneath each fuselage and there were twin tail-wheels, the last on an Air Force aircraft.

Armament consisted of six .50-caliber fixed guns with 400rpg in the wing center section. Wing racks could carry four drop tanks, up to 6,000lb (2,727kg) of bombs or 25 rockets, or a center pod containing eight more guns. Power was provided by Packard Merlin V-1650-23/25 engines with "handed" propellers rotating in opposite directions to avoid excessive torque on take-off. The USAAF placed an order for 500 P-82B fighters but only 20 had been built when the war ended in August 1945. The Twin Mustang did figure when post-war procurement was revived, serving in limited numbers as an escort fighter and night fighter.

Although it was to see minor action in numerous small post-war conflicts, the Mustang had one more major war to fight. Between 1950 and 1952, during the Korean War, Mustangs flew 62,607 sorties and 194 P-51s were lost to enemy action on missions that were primarily for ground support. It was fitting that the North American F-86 Sabre followed on from the Mustang, which on January 23, 1953, ceased combat in Korea.

Aircraft Walkaround

Above: *Instrument panel, P-51D. Instruments on this panel included the remote reading compass indicator; manifold pressure gauge; airspeed indicator; directional gyro; artificial horizon; coolant temperature gauge; RPM gauge; rate-of-climb indicator.*

Above: *The second Mustang I at Mines Field, Los Angeles in the summer of 1941. The Mustang III (British equivalent to the P-51B/C) entered service with the RAF in February 1944 when it began equipping 19 Squadron at Ford.*

Top right: *P-51C-10 "INA The Macon Belle" owned by Kermit Weeks which in WWII was flown by Lt Lee Archer Jr. in the 302nd FS, 332nd FG, Ramitelli, Italy.*

Opposite page, above: *P-51A Mustang "Mrs Virginia" is a rare Allison-powered Mustang and is operated by the Planes of Fame Museum at Chino, California.*

Opposite page, below: *P-51C A4-2 in the colors of the 99th FS, 322nd FG "Red Tails," operated by the Tuskegee Airmen at Ramitelli, Italy, in late 1944.*

Left: *Port gun bay in P-51B "Princess Elizabeth." For the four .50 Brownings to fit in the wings of the P-51B they had to be canted at an angle, with the ammunition belts feeding over and down into the breeches.*

Right: *Expanded view of the gun bay on P-51B "Princess Elizabeth." A, B, and C models carried four .50-caliber Browning machine guns, two in each wing. These were mounted slightly leaning over in the gun bays allowing easier flow of the ammunition.*

Below: *The main undercarriage wheel well of the P-51 Mustang contains a mass of piping. The two clam shell doors, which cover the wheels when in flight, are operated in sequence. They remain down when the aircraft is at rest due to the absence of pressure in the hydraulic system.*

Above: *Early models of the Mustang featured a "high-back" fuselage, with a framed cockpit canopy, as here, on P-51C 43-25147 "Princess Elizabeth." Pilots found that the rearward view from the cockpit was restricted. A three-blade Aeroproducts propeller with broad hollow blades saved several pounds over the four-blade Hamilton gear.*

SIGHT LINE MARK

250 YDS - 70⁹⁄₁₆ FOR INB'D GUN
₵ AIRPLANE   300 YDS - 72 FOR INB'D GUN
PLUMB BOB LINE   MAX. INDICATED AIR SPEED
                                    250 YDS-76¹³⁄₁₆ FOR OUT B'D GUN   328 M.P.H., SET AIRPLANE
                                    300 YDS-78¹³⁄₁₆ FOR OUT B'D GUN   LEVEL LUGS 0° 30' 00" NOSE
                                                                            UP

SPECIAL • INSTRUCTIONS

A. GUNS MUST HAVE OIL BUFFER CYLINDER FILLED WITH OIL OF U.S. ARMY SPEC. 2-36D "OIL RECOIL LIGHT"
B. GUNS MUST BE SPARINGLY LUBRICATED WITH OIL OF SPEC. AXS-777 WITH MIN. LUBRICATION ON FIR-
   ING PIN AND FIRING PIN WELL
C. ON MISSIONS REQUIRING GUN HEAT, HEATERS MUST BE TURNED ON IMMEDIATELY AFTER STARTING ENG.

ELECT
TERM

Right: *P-51D in flight showing the scoop beneath. Studies revealed that the optimum location for the Merlin version's intercooler radiator on the XP-51B was found to be beneath the fuselage, just aft of the cockpit. Externally the P-51B differed little from the P-51A. The nose was fatter, with the dorsal air scoop replaced by a less obvious ventral intake behind the spinner.*

Below: *P-51D in the colors of "Sizzlin' Liz" flown in World War II by Major Gerald E. "Monty" Mongomery in the 4th Fighter Group at Debden.*

Opposite page, right: *P-51D Mustang "Double Trouble Two." The colors are those of the 353rd Fighter Group.*

Opposite page, far right: *Via field modifications, the RAF removed the original NAA three-panel hinged canopy and replaced it with a one-piece tear-drop sliding canopy, which could be opened in flight and on the landing approach in bad weather.*

Opposite page, below: *P-51D 44-13903 "Glamorous Gal." The P-51D was practically identical to the P-51K apart from a propeller change.*

Col. E.H.Beverly
C.C. L.L.Lang
A.C.SGT.J.Royston

AAF.SPEC.PROJ.NO.92778
U.S. ARMY P-51D-5-NA
SERIAL NO. AAF 44-13903

CREW WEIGHT 200 LBS.

SERVICE THIS AIRPLANE WITH
GRADE 100/130 FUEL. IF NOT
AVAILABLE TO 06-5-1 WILL BE
CONSULTED FOR EMERGENCY ACTION

SUITABLE FOR AROMATIC FUEL

Opposite page, far left: *On the right side of the P-51D cockpit, the green oxygen hose leads to the oxygen regulator. The switch panel to the right of that includes the ammeter dial plus the battery and generator disconnect switches. To the right of the pilot's seat with red buttons on top is the VHF radio control box and aft of that is the IFF (identification friend or foe) radar control panel.*

Opposite page, left: *The Mk VIII reflector gunsight and the simple ring and post were the two gunsights fitted to the majority of USAAF fighters before the K-14/K-14A gyro computing sight was introduced in spring 1944. Based on the British gyroscopic Mk IIC/IID, it gave very accurate deflection shooting.*

Top right: *Two of the most famous fighter groups in the MTO and in the ETO were the red-tailed 322nd Fighter Group known as the "Tuskegee Airmen" and the 4th Fighter Group at Debden; P-51D VF-G NL10601 of the Confederate Air Force (now Commemorative Air Force) is painted in the latter's colors.*

Opposite page, bottom: *Extensive redesign resulted in six .50-caliber machine guns on the P-51D; all upright instead of canted, which virtually eliminated feed stoppages. The two inboard guns had 400 rounds each, while the other four each had 270 rounds.*

Lower right: *P-5lD-20 44-63864 "Twilight Tear" was assigned to 1st Lieutenant Hubert "Bill" Davis in the 83rd Fighter Squadron, 78th Fighter Group, at Duxford three weeks after the group had made the transition from P-47s to P-51s. Davis flew the bulk of his thirty-five combat missions in it, scoring three aerial victories in March 1945.*

Above: *P-51D-20-NA 44-14561 at Duxford painted in wartime colors to represent P-51D CY-D "Velma" flown by Captain Frank E. Birtviel in the 343rd Fighter Squadron, 55th Fighter Group. All of his Mustangs were named after his sweetheart and future wife, Miss Velma Randolph.*

Left: *P-51D Mustang line-up at the world-famous Flying Legends Air Show at the IWM, Duxford with "Big Beautiful Doll" and "Old Crow" nearest the camera. P-51D 44-14450 B6-S "Old Crow" was the favorite mount of Captain Clarence E. "Bud" Anderson in the 363rd Fighter Squadron, 357th Fighter Group, at Leiston, Suffolk.*

Right: *Trials showed the later bubble canopy brought no significant deterioration in the aircraft's handling characteristics and experienced pilots were hugely impressed with the improved view, though many still liked to have a rear-view mirror for quick "clear my-six" checks.*

Below: *"Big Beautiful Doll" displays its beautiful clean lines and laminar flow wing. A Hamilton four-bladed propeller on the P-51D replaced the bladed one and the radiator under the mid-fuselage was deeper.*

PART 2
The Missions

Preparation for a Mission

Taking the teletype, the group intelligence duty officer glances at the words on the yellow paper before signing for the message. "Okay, sergeant," he says and almost before the teletype man is gone, the duty intelligence officer (IO) is back in his sack. The message is a warning order—an official tip that higher headquarters is considering a bomber escort mission to the Nuremburg area the next morning. But it is only 22:45 hours and the plan can be changed a dozen times before the fighters actually take off. The IO goes to sleep.

Two hours later the sergeant shakes him again and hands over another message—the field order. A glance reveals that the show is definitely on, with the Fighter Group to be escorting bombers. The S-2 officer stumbles from his bunk and rouses the duty operations officer. Together they start making detailed plans for the group's part in the mission. Using data from the field order, they plot the course from Duxford to the rendezvous point and then on with the bombers into the target and back out again. They calculate flying time to the rendezvous and figure when pilots will have to start the engines of their checker-nosed planes. They schedule briefing for an hour before that. Then they telephone the three squadron intelligence officers on call at the officers' club quarters. The squadron S-2s will pass the information along to the men in their outfits—enlisted men and pilots.

The duty IO begins marking the course on the briefing room's big front-wall map. Red string for the fighters, blue string for the bombers they are to escort. Then he turns to a small sideboard, where he pins up

Above: Armorers and mechanics in a hangar at East Wretham in 1944 watch as a P-51D fighter of the 359th Fighter Group is towed into position by a Cle-Track vehicle.

parallel rows of Flying Fortresses and fighter silhouettes, each numbered to represent a different group. Just to make sure there is no slip-up, tail and wing cut-outs show unit markings of each bomber outfit.

On another board the IO chalks up a schedule showing when to start engines, when to take off, when to set course, when to rendezvous, and when to do a lot of other things. This board is the timetable for the mission, a timetable which must be followed to the minute if the fighters are to do their assigned job.

As the IO winds up his work on the briefing boards, squadron company quartermasters (CQs) are stirring from the orderly rooms and awakening ground men-mechanics, armorers, radio men, and others. Engineering and armament sections turn out in strength. Without eating breakfast, two men for each ship—a mechanic and an armorer—grab bicycles or climb into trucks and ride out to the waiting fighters. Others hurry to the mess hall to eat breakfast and then relieve those who went first to the planes.

But things are not going so smoothly at every dispersal area. While performing the pre-flight checks, one crew chief has found that a badly worn part must be replaced or his plane will not be able to fly the mission. He phones his flight chief at the hangar and explains his trouble. The flight chief steps over to the tech supply facility to draw a new part and the supply man spends a couple of minutes finding it. Three or four minutes later the flight chief is at the plane with the part. Time is short, and the mechanics work fast but carefully to make the replacement. Then they slap on the engine cowling and buckle it down. The flight chief himself decides to pre-flight the craft to see if the new part corrects the trouble. It does, and the gasoline truck wheels up again. Although the tanks were filled after the first pre-flight, the second warm-up took several gallons and on a long mission those few gallons may mean the difference between a pilot getting back or going down.

Left, lower left and below right: *The 353rd Fighter Group briefing officer points to the next target for a group of assembled Mustang pilots in England. Information display boards give the various code words to use in radio communication, weather details, flare colors, and check-point times. Below we see Mustang pilots in the 4th Fighter Group at Debden (left) and the 53rd Fighter Group pilots at Raydon undergoing briefings.*

Only a handful of communications men get up and they merely stand by the aircraft in case unexpected faults develop in the radio equipment. The radio section has worked late the night before, pre-flighting transmitters and receivers after yesterday's mission landed and the airways were clear of combat messages.

Meanwhile group and squadron S-2 and S-3 sections are still working. At the briefing room intelligence men are gathering odd bits of information, such as the latest flak reports, and posting it on the briefing map. Operations clerks are making final checks with squadrons on what planes are to be used for the mission, who will fly each one, and what aircraft have been put in commission overnight.

After gathering data from their engineering departments on what planes will be ready for the mission, squadron S-3 sections relay the data to group S-3 and then relax. Their job, except for carting pilots out to their planes after briefing, is over. Squadron intelligence staffs, however, are kept busy preparing course cards and individual maps for pilots to take with them. Here, as in everything else connected with the combat operation, accuracy is essential. A wrong compass bearing on a course card or a slight error in the rendezvous point on the map may throw the entire mission into confusion.

A tug on the shoulder by the squadron CQs bring the pilots abruptly out of sleep's oblivion. Some may be feeling the strain of combat and the relaxation that follows. The thoughts running through George Preddy's mind on August 6, 1944, were typical: "Do I feel rough. Stomach churning. Great party! Too much to drink. That $1200 pot I won will help the Group out in the Bond drive. Bed at 4:00, Up at 8:30. As soon as the briefing is over I'll have to cure my hangover with some deep gulps of pure oxygen before takeoff time."

Then the voice comes. "Wake up, Sir: breakfast at oh-eight-thirty; briefing at oh-nine hundred." It is the same thing at the same time every morning, seven days a week. The CQ removes his torch from the pilot's face and moves further up the hut to repeat the performance at another bed. A couple of the gang are still asleep. They will miss breakfast and catch the truck for briefing half way down the drive. Within a few minutes pilots are putting on their "long johns," khaki ODs, tie, wool sweater, wool-lined khaki jacket, and heavy wool socks and some, their beloved RAF flying boots; snazzy, ox-blood colored, lined with trimmed sheep fur and very warm. One boot has a small pocket that contains a beautiful little pearl-handled, single-bladed knife with which to cut off the tops. Still, some wear the heavy, GI-issue high-topped shoes that the Gestapo can spot a mile away. Sunglasses are a must. Lastly, pick up the "ratty" cap, put it on at a slightly rakish angle, and head for the door. As they strap on their wristwatches they note the time is just past 08.00 hours.

Washed and shaved, the pilots make their way on foot from the squadron location along another path to the communal site and to the long building that is the mess hall. There is a blackout, so the only lights come from flashlights stabbing through the darkness. Cigarettes glow; talk is muted. It is hard to feel hungry, partly because of the hour and partly because of the nervous gut feeling about the mission. "Where are we going? How much time have we got till start engines? Is this another lousy milk run?"

Inside the well-lit and warm mess hall all is light and noise. A bedlam greets the arrivals as they enter the door and the smoke of burning grease assails the nostrils and smarts in their eyes as they file in for real fresh eggs and perhaps a slice or two of salty bacon, plus cereal and black coffee. Fresh eggs confirm that a combat mission is in the offing and the first problem is, can you get them down? After a drink of grapefruit or tomato juice or coffee it usually becomes easier, but each mouthful becomes an additional lump of lead in the pit of the stomach.

Normally the only eggs available are the dehydrated variety, which come in square boxes. These are prepared by being whipped into a great

Above: *Flying suit worn by Lieutenant Thompson in the 436th Fighter Squadron, 479th "Riddle's Raiders" Fighter Group at Wattisham, Suffolk, England.*

sticky emulsion and then apparently fried in axle grease left over from the needs of the motor pool; the result is a well-vulcanized, plastic lump of lukewarm goo. Milk also is available only in powdered form. Sometimes pilots eat oatmeal and powdered milk—not because they like it but because it is warm and filling. Food is prepared to eliminate indigestion and sickness at high altitude and, anyway, it could be the last meal for quite some time and one might have to walk home. Bacon, orange juice, toast, fruit, pancakes, and SOS ("shit-on-a-shingle," creamed beef on toast) are available.

There is very little conversation at the table. Just drink your coffee and pick at the food. The coffee tastes of rust. Casual conversation swells; no one speculates about the mission ahead although the volume of engine noise high above indicates a bomber escort. Then it is back out into the dark and the cold morning. A grey light has started to fill the sky in the east.

By 08:50 hours fifty young pilots have climbed on to the back of four "Six by Six" trucks waiting outside the mess hall and head for briefing. After a half-mile of winding roads the trucks reach the large assembly of buildings beside the airfield and stop outside a Quonset complex. The occupants of the trucks tumble out and make for the open double doors, passing through the open blackout curtains into a hall way. Everyone crowds around a small table where two clerks check off each man's name, allowing him to proceed through the adjacent door into the briefing room. An MP stands guard to see that no unauthorized personnel gain admittance.

The station weather officer steps to the front. All night, observers and forecasters have been making regular readings on temperature, wind velocity and direction, and other factors. Adding this local data to teletype reports from other stations, the weather officers tell the fliers what to expect in the way of clouds and winds at varying altitudes along their route, and at what altitude condensation trails will appear. The weather en route will be good and the weather at home base will remain CAVU (Ceiling and Visibility Unlimited).

The weatherman's briefing is short. The mission leader takes over. He may be the group commander, the deputy commander, or a squadron CO, but, regardless of his rank or position otherwise, today he must

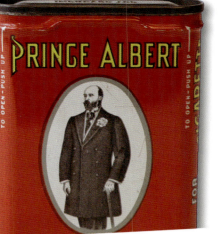

Right: Prince Albert Crimp Cut long-burning pipe and cigarette tobacco tin; the brand was commonly smoked by USAAF personnel.

ensure that everything goes according to the field order and he commands unquestioned obedience. He has studied the teletype carefully and has noted any flak areas or enemy airfields that may need attention along the route. He relays all this to the men who will fly with him and also calls their attention to other information on the briefing boards and the wall map. When he has finished, he asks intelligence and operations officers if they have anything to add. They haven't.

Pilots have been silently attentive during briefing. To most of them it is an old story, set today in a new pattern. With that the colonel looks at his watch and says, in a low voice, "Hack watches!" Pilots set the fluorescent hand on their military issue watches, leave the stem out, and listen to the count-down, "Ten, nine, eight, seven, six, five, four, three, two, one, Hack!" They snap the stem in and watch the second hand begin to track on the black face of their watches. Then the "Exec" shouts; "Ten-shun!" and they all stand. The CO says, "Dismissed!" There is a rush for the door; they have to fight their way through the crowd.

As the pilots leave the briefing room a sergeant, standing in the doorway, gives each one a Mission Data Card on which are carried the radio call signs and other signals information for the day, plus crucial times and checkpoints. Some of this is given in coded form as the cards will be carried for reference on the flight and there is always the possibility that this information may fall into enemy hands early in the mission.

They make for their squadron ready-rooms and the personal equipment store with lockers. Some are taking a last smoke, some are joking, others are quietly going about their business. They take off their B-15 jackets and climb into corset-like Berger "G-suits," putting them on over their GI trousers. The G-suits, as well as the parachutes they will pick

Feeding the Pilots

Breakfasts were nourishing, though not elegant—in wartime England meals seldom were. Typically the breakfast menu, like those for other meals, rotated. One morning the main course might be chipped beef in thick white gravy on a slice of toast made from heavy brown English bread, marmalade and coffee. In the dining room, white cotton tablecloths covered each table, on which sat utilitarian salt and peppershakers, a bowl of sugar, a can of Pet evaporated milk with two holes punched in the top, and various condiments.

Left and below: An airbase dining hall was functional, filled with rows of long, serviceable tables and benches. The "meat can" was the standard eating receptacle of the US soldier. The aluminium M1932 version was later replaced by the corrosion-resistant stainless steel M1942 version.

up later, the collapsible dinghies waiting in the planes, and the orange-colored "Mae Wests" have been checked by the base personal equipment section and by squadron parachute men.

Next comes the Summer Flying Suit—a one-piece coverall garment, which is almost standard wear despite it being far from summer weather. Zipped up, each pilot then goes through the careful procedure of placing specific items in certain pockets. Then it is out to the planes in "Six by Six" trucks and Dodge Command cars. Mechanics climb on the wings to give the airmen a hand up.

While a pilot settles in the cockpit fastening his safety harness, connecting his oxygen mask and radio cable, he jokes with the mechanic and asks how the plane checked out on the pre-flight inspection. He glances up and down the line at other ships, takes a quick look at his wrist watch. Suddenly earphones crackle with a message from the tower announcing that engine start is delayed. This can often happen when the bombers to be escorted are late in meeting their own formation assembly

Above: *De-briefing at a base in East Anglia following a mission. A tot of rum or whiskey helped loosen tongues and intelligence officers could pump the pilots for information gained on the mission.*

Left: *Page Witold Lanowski (right) and another Polish pilot in the RAF who flew with the 354th Fighter Group discuss the troublesome ammunition feeds with an squadron armorer.*

lines. Sometimes the delay is only a few minutes; on other occasions a half-hour or more. The crew chief, recognizing his pilot's unease at this time, makes small talk, mostly about his experiences on a recent two-day pass to London. But the delay is short; the earphones crackle again; revised engine start is 09:50 hours. The crew chief closes the canopy. The pilot locks it.

"Chocks are out whenever you're ready," shouts the crew chief. Pilots look over the switches and instrument panel again mentally rechecking all previous moves. It's time!

The crew chief slides down off the wing. As the pilot goes through the engine starting procedure he hears the splutter of a Merlin nearby as another pilot beats the clock. The crew chief has already run the engine so it is warm and only a second's priming is required. As the inertia starter begins its whine, the mechanics jump from the wings and stand away from the prop and the wing tips.

"Clear!" yells the pilot.

"Clear!" echoes the crew chief. The engine roars and settles down to a steady rumble. Mechanics, armorers, and one or two radio men are out to watch the fighters taxi into position and take off.

Across the field in the control tower, a corporal with binoculars calls out each plane's letter markings, as it becomes airborne and a private chalks up the plane takeoff time on a blackboard. Below and to one side of the control tower, medics in an ambulance and firemen in a hose wagon watch sharply as the fighters roll down the grass runway and struggle into the air. There is no business for them today.

The ground men watch for a while and then start sweating out the mission. They pick up scattered tools and cleaning rods and then get another pair of wing tanks ready to fit under each plane as soon as the mission returns. Gradually they drift towards the nearby shacks. Again they play cards, read, talk, or sleep.

As the planes head out, only the control tower and the direction-finding station have contact with the mission and they will be called a couple of thousand feet above the bombers, which are ahead and to his right. During the mission many pilots talk to their planes—cursing them, praising them. It would make fascinating reading to record a five-hour mission in the cockpit of a Mustang—but it would be unprintable.

Everyone is on hand when they return—crew chiefs and their assistants, armorers, radio men, fuel and oil men with their trucks, flight chiefs in each section, flight surgeons, MPs on each side of the runway where it crosses the perimeter track, firemen, medics and their ambulance, and anyone else who happens to be around.

Signaled in from the tower, the planes peel off, circle and land. As soon as a plane stops at its dispersal area the crew hops on to the wings and checks with the pilot on its performance in the air. "Did you get any Krauts? Was the engine all right? Did the guns fire all right? Was the radio reception clear? Did everything go okay?" Regardless of his answers, the

Right: Radio Mechanic and A.P. (Airplane) Armorer proficiency medal.

the compartments of the planes which fired. As mechanics and armorers wind up their jobs the radio men take over. By now all the 8th Air Force fighters and bombers have settled at their home fields and the airwaves are clear of combat messages, so communications men can test transmitters and receivers.

Men in the air engineering squadron are also on the case. That plane which caught the flak today will need a new wing, and their job is to change it. On checking the craft for other damage, they find a few small holes in the tail that will need a sheet metal specialist's attention. They will be working a few days on this one plane, plus any others that are seriously damaged in the meantime.

And as the engineering men line up their repair jobs the pilots report to their squadron IOs for interrogation. IOs gather claims and other data from individual pilots and phone it to the group S-2, who compiles it into a composite report he telephones to higher headquarters. Enlisted men collect maps and file them away. The pilots, hungry and fatigued, hurry to chow as soon as they leave interrogation. They discuss the mission in minute detail, comparing performances of their different planes, speculating about Luftwaffe tactics, observing that bomber losses were light today.

Squadron engineering sections are consulting with flight chiefs to find which planes are due for routine inspections, which ones require minor repairs overnight, which will be out of action longer, and so

Above: P-51Ds of the 78th Fighter Group at Duxford, Cambridgeshire, at the end of the war. A 16-plane squadron would be airborne in four minutes and a three-squadron group of 48 in 13 minutes.

ground men set to work as the pilot goes to interrogation. Gasoline and oil trucks make their rounds. Crewmen clean guns, look for oil leaks, inspect tires, and take care of countless other details.

Any defect reported by the pilot gets extra attention and double checking before the crew leaves for the barracks. Wing tanks for tomorrow's mission are fitted in place and new ammunition is loaded into

on. Squadron operations takes this data and passes it along to group operations, which in turn transmits it to higher headquarters. The latter will use the data in determining how many planes are available for tomorrow's mission. Group engineering works with squadron engineering sections and group operations and also reports to higher headquarters. Within a few hours, today's mission is a part of the past and a good bit of the ground work has been laid for tomorrow's. The night-duty men turn to their routine tasks, read magazines, or write home. The rest of the station relaxes.

Big Friends, Little Friends

"Soon we saw three P-51s to one side and above, those loveable sonsabitches! ... Our escort soon left us, however, as in the logistics of P-51 fuel economy versus B-24 fuel economy, a P-51 could go fairly far afield but not for long and not at our comparative caterpillar's speed."

—Bob Shaver, 389th "Sky Scorpions" Bomb Group, October 7, 1944, mission to Kassel

In the ETO in 1943 escorting US fighter pilots were not allowed to chase enemy pilots who attacked the B-17s and B-24s—the "Big Friends"—but simply drive fighters away and then return to the bomber formations. Colonel Hubert "Hub" Zemke, commanding the 56th Fighter Group that was equipped with P-47 Thunderbolts, knew that fighter pilots could not just fly close to bombers at slow speeds and wait for the enemy. His strategy was that once an enemy was seen, fighter pilots had to engage and pursue them, break up their formation before they reached the bombers and destroy them.

General Ira C. Eaker, commanding 8th Air Force said, that when British-made 108-gallon (491-liter) paper drop tanks were made available they would permit "long-range accompanying missions in force and continuity of operations." William E. Kepner, commander of VIII Fighter Command, declared that since 300 miles (482km) was about the maximum range for a P-47 "some longer ranged fighter is necessary." Kepner required eight groups of P-47s and ten groups of P-38s or P-51s, "or a combination of both. Thus, a Ramrod [a bomber and escort mission] of over 500 miles [805km] would require 18 groups." Eaker however, preferred the P-38 Lightning to the P-47 and P-51, and others saw the P-51B as a tactical, ground-support fighter. In October 1943, despite

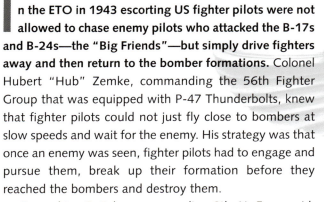

Left: Two P-51D Mustangs fly close escort for B-17G "Sentimental Journey" over the Gulf of Mexico.

protestations from Kepner, Eaker decided to give the P-51Bs to the 9th Air Force, which was to receive eight Mustang groups. The first to arrive, in November 1943, was the 354th Fighter Group, which was to be based at Boxted.

On December 1, P-51Bs of the 354th Fighter Group flew their first mission, a sweep over Belgium. Twelve days later Mustangs carrying external tanks flew their first long-range escort mission—490 miles (789km) to Kiel and back. On December 16, 1943, 1st Lieutenant Charles F. Gumm Jr., of the 354th Fighter Group made the first Mustang kill in the ETO when he downed a Bf 109.

"By January 1944," states the official AAF history, "the value of the P-51 as a long-range escort fighter plane had become so apparent that the principles on which allocations had been made in the theater between the 8th and 9th Air Forces were completely revised." The second Mustang group in England was the 357th, which had six P-51Bs by Christmas Day. The third P-51 group was the 363rd, which arrived that Christmas and received its P-51Bs in January 1944. On January 24, British and US commanders reached an agreement that placed most of the P-51 units in the 8th Air Force. Four days later the 357th Fighter Group was traded to the 8th Air Force for the P-47-equipped 358th Fighter Group, which became part of IX Fighter Command. Eventually, the 8th would be equipped almost exclusively with the P-51s, with the P-47s and P-38s being transferred to the 9th Air Force.

The "Pioneer Mustang" Group

Richard E. Turner was assigned to the new 354th Fighter Group at Tonopah, Nevada. In England the pilots were sent to Greenham Common airdrome in Berkshire to cut their teeth on the P-51As of the 10th Reconnaissance Group. Within a week every pilot was checked out and they entrained again, to Colchester where they were loaded into trucks and transported to Boxted.

"The 356th Fighter Squadron's flight commanders, O'Connor, Goodnight, Lamb and I, all bunked in one hut with Jim Howard, the Squadron CO and Bob Brooks our Operations Officer, plus a few assorted new pilots. The arrangement proved to be an excellent one for coordination and control of the squadron, enabling us to exercise flexibility and to respond instantly to any order handed to the squadron from Group.

"Our first month in the ETO was spent flying our new P-51s on training missions over England. We concentrated on Squadron and Group control missions while practicing mutual support tactics with the traditional combat units of an element of two fighters, a flight of four, a squadron of sixteen and a group of forty-eight fighters. At the same time, we developed and practiced the technique and deployment tactics necessary to provide protective escort to bombers."

On December 1, 1943, the 354th Fighter Group flew its first combat mission, a fighter sweep over St-Omer, designed to introduce it to German flak and enemy territory. For this initial mission the 8th Air Force had sent the group Lieutenant Colonel Don Blakeslee from the veteran 4th Fighter Group, which had evolved from the "Eagle" Squadron composed of Americans flying with the British before the American entry into the war. Blakeslee briefed and led them on this crucial flight. "He was all business and the business was killing," recalled Richard E. Turner. "In the briefing he let us know that he was a master of my craft; and that he would brook nothing less than perfection from those who flew with him. After briefing was concluded Blakeslee discussed the standard tactics to be used in the event of engagement with enemy aircraft. After emphasizing the mutual support positions and breaking movements he stressed the inflexible policy of American pilots in the case of head-on attack between fighters. He stated in no uncertain terms that we were never, repeat NEVER, to turn away from head-on attack before the enemy!

"An hour and a half after take-off we arrived back at base without casualty except for a flak hole Jim Lane collected from one of the bursts we had seen. The only real excitement on the mission came at landing when one of the group cut Colonel Blakeslee out of the traffic pattern and the Colonel informed one and all that 'the next SOB that cuts in front of him while landing was going to get an ass full of lead'. Following this terse little announcement there wasn't a P-51 to be found in the pattern until Blakeslee had landed and taxied into the hardstand.

"In debriefing Colonel Blakeslee observed that, considering all aspects of our first mission, we might survive the war, providing we learned to land after missions in an orderly manner rather than the method of 'God save the hindmost'. For three days after our first mission on December 1 we flew further training missions over England practicing our air work, and formation. Also instruments and, needless to say, working extra hard on landing pattern traffic control.

"During our early days of combat we had become quickly accustomed to the fact that our long-range escort missions called for up to five hours of sitting in the cramped cockpit of the Mustang fighters. The discomfort we

Above: Richard E. Turner of the 354th Fighter Group (group badge at top).

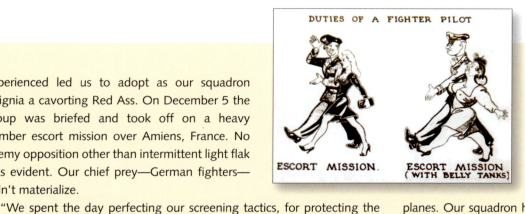

experienced led us to adopt as our squadron insignia a cavorting Red Ass. On December 5 the group was briefed and took off on a heavy bomber escort mission over Amiens, France. No enemy opposition other than intermittent light flak was evident. Our chief prey—German fighters—didn't materialize.

"We spent the day perfecting our screening tactics, for protecting the bomber stream. I gained a new and deep respect for the bomber crews as I watched them plow doggedly through flak concentrations without wavering. As I watched this same display of perseverance almost daily in the months to come it became my firm conviction that bomber crews as a whole must be unrivaled for sheer guts and determination.

"Flak was the one danger we couldn't help them with and from what I saw they simply ignored it if that was possible. Due to their massiveness bombers couldn't make quick and erratic maneuvers so they took a calculated risk and flew straight on course through the black hell. The action was inspiring and impressive for an escorting fighter and I have entertained nothing but genuine admiration for bomber crews since. Our

second mission ended as another 'milk run'—a term we came to use describing missions with no claims, no losses and no enemy action. I began to wonder where the enemy fighters were hiding.

"March ended our fourth month of combat and the group had flown 45 combat missions, had shot down 159 Germans and lost 45 men and 47 planes. Our squadron had accounted for about a third of the victories and lost only four pilots in combat, a record we were justly proud of. We were determined to maintain this trend and high score. The 356th Squadron ultimately destroyed 298 German aircraft, losing only twenty-two pilots in combat and training accidents—a kill/loss ratio of better than 13 to 1. As far as I knew this is the finest record ever achieved by an Air Force squadron in continual combat for over an eighteen-month period and I am understandably proud to have been with such an outstanding group of men."

Above: A wry US "escort mission" cartoon.
Below: The "Iowa Beaut" in the 355th Fighter Group flown by Lieutenant Robert Hulderman tags along on a practice mission flown by Flying Fortresses of the 381st Bomb Group at Ridgewell.

Escort Mission

Late in November 1944, 27-year old 1st Lieutenant George Vanden Heuvel in the 376th Fighter Squadron, 361st Fighter Group, at Little Walden was one of the escort pilots for the "Big Friends" attacking oil and transport-ation targets. Just north of the Dutch town of Zwolle at 11:24 hours, through the haze the familiar shapes of Liberators appeared, two groups in trail, about sixty aircraft. A half-hour later the radio suddenly sprang to life: "'Leader to all Glowbright aircraft: bandits at 9 o'clock low. Two large gaggles northeast of Ulzen.'

"'Jeepers, look at them, there must be a couple of hundred', someone excitedly exclaimed. I instantly dropped my hand to switch the fuel selector to main tanks and then pulled the salvo handles just below the throttle control to jettison the drop tanks. Immediately there was a slight jump in airspeed and this quickly advanced as I pushed the throttle to the full open position in an effort to stay with White 3, who was diving to intercept the enemy horde that appeared to be making straight for the bombers. There were well over 100 single-engine fighters in mass formation and it was obvious that eight Mustangs would be unable to deflect this force.

"I picked out an Fw 190 about 1,000ft [305m] below, diving away. Pushing the throttle lever up to the stop, I attempted to overhaul the enemy who was increasing his angle of dive. Three or four seconds into the descent and I felt a slight vibration in the stick. A quick look at the airspeed indicator showed the needle pointer climbing past 420mph [676kmph], which was over 530mph [853kmph] true airspeed at this altitude. Now the stick began to resist my hand pressure and moved back and forth in a way I could not control.

"As a result of this compressibility, the nose of my Mustang pitched up and down. I smartly chopped the throttle to cut power. Still the Mustang headed down in a vice-like grip, resisting all attempts to move the stick. The altimeter unwound rapidly: 15,000-, 14,000-, 13,000-, 12,000ft [4,572, 4,267, 3,962, 3,658m]. At last, as the Mustang cut into denser air some feel returned to the controls. Finally, around 10,000ft [3,048m] *Mary Mine*'s nose started to come up and presented me with a horizon. Despite wearing a G-suit, the stress on my body was such that I momentarily

Above: P-51D "Yellow Jackets" in the 361st Fighter Group in formation. One of the P-51Ds is 44-13926 E2-S, being flown by the group's third-ranking ace, 1st Lieutenant Urban Drew.

'blacked out'. Spots passed before my eyes. I looked at the altimeter and saw that I had dropped from 26,000ft [7,925m] to recover at 9,000ft [2,743m].

"Opening the throttle, I climbed towards heavy contrails away to the south, curving in a wide spiral to try and keep a true airspeed in excess of 250mph [402kmph]. Being alone, it was necessary to keep a constant lookout for a surprise attack from above. As 19,000ft [5,791m] was reached, I saw aircraft approaching at roughly the same altitude from the east. As a precaution, I leveled out and turned in towards them. I soon identified them as Fw 190s at *Staffel* strength—a dozen or more. Alarmed, I pushed the throttle 'through the gate,' breaking the safety wire to gain emergency power and called for assistance over the radio: 'This is Yorkshire White 4. I need help. Angels 17. South of Ulzen'.

"I turned in behind one of the Focke-Wulfs, framed the enemy in the K-14 computing gunsight and adjusted the throttle grip until the six diamond pips on the reflector plate matched the wingspan of the Fw 190. I pressed the trigger on the stick. Immediately I felt the Mustang yaw to the left. I brought the fighter's nose back towards the target and fired again. Once more my aircraft skid left. I realized that only one of the six guns was

working: there was no point in continuing the attack. White puffs of time-fused cannon shells alerted me to break away. Even so, as I leveled out in an attempt to run for it, Focke-Wulfs came in to attack from both flanks.

"Fear tightened my stomach, but my instant reaction was to avoid the cannon shells and bullets that would be unleashed at *Mary Mine* in a fraction of a second. I made an abrupt left forward movement of the stick and the

Left and below: 361st Fighter Group art work on the walls at Bottisham airfield, Cambridgeshire.

Mustang sliced over and down into a Split-S (a roll over into a dive, reversing direction of travel). I glanced upwards and was amazed to see both enemy aircraft disintegrating in flames: one that had been closing in, in an inverted position had slammed into the other."

Relieved to find himself alone again, "Van" once more recovered to a higher altitude along the bomber track. At 22,000ft (6,706m) specks ahead became single-engined Fw 190s maneuvering to attack a distant group of B-24s. In the hope of dispersing the enemy, Van turned in behind one. His intended victim flew on a steady course, apparently unaware of the danger coming up behind. Van pressed the gun trigger. Once more only a single weapon fired, pulling the P-51's nose left. Van decided to disengage before again becoming a target for the enemy. Diving away to use the momentum to gain high altitude, the engine coolant and oil temperature gauges both showed readings in excess of the permissible maximum—past the red warning lines. Alarmed, Van realized that he still had the throttle right forward in the War Emergency Power position and quickly retarded it. He checked the setting of the radiator scoop doors for maximum cooling, but these were already fully open. After a few minutes he made out the shape of the Zuider Zee.

The 361st Group tentatively claimed 23 enemy aircraft shot down for one loss. Most of the enemy aircraft destroyed were the Fw 190s of an assault group caught while attacking the B-24s. His intelligence reports given, Van was transported to his quarters where, after freshening up, he went to the Officers' Club to join other pilots in talking over details of the successful mission.

Above: P-51D "Dear Arabella" in the 361st Fighter Group with underwing tanks, peeling away. The tanks had a major effect on the tactical applications of the Mustang, dramatically extending the range of the fighter on long-range bomber escort missions.

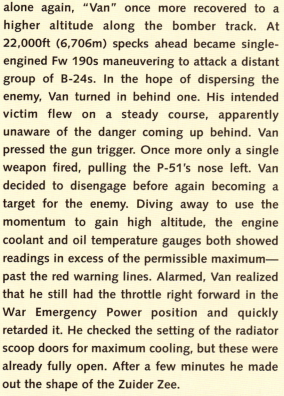

Coup de Grace

Lieutenant Kenneth H. French, a bombardier in the 490th Bomb Group, recalled a mission on November 21, 1944. "Our briefed target for today was a synthetic oil refinery at Lützkendorf, about 8 miles [13km] from Merseburg. Bad weather had been forecast in front of us and even though we had climbed to 28,500ft [8,687m] to try to get over it we still ran into it when we reached about 8° E. The 1st Division also went to the same target today. They went in first at a bombing altitude believed to have been 21,000ft [6,400m] or less. Fighters hit them between the clouds and we were told that about 20 bombers were shot down. Our escort of P-51s took out 60 enemy fighters. Nearing the target, we received a call that there were fighters in the area but none attacked us."

In early 1945 the "Little Friends"—as the bomber crews called their fighter escorts—racked up high scores of downed enemy fighters. On Sunday, January 14, 1945, a force of 187 Fortresses in the 1st Division was escorted by forty-two Mustangs that battled with about 250 enemy fighters, claiming about one hundred kills. Four groups on fighter sweeps engaged more than 150 fighters, claiming over forty destroyed. Norman K. Andrew, a B-17 navigator in the 487th Bomb Group, went to Magdeburg, and subsequently recalled: "About 50 miles [80km] past Hamburg I saw four P-51s drop their tanks and peel off. One strafed a railroad. Couldn't see the other three. About a minute after they went down the *Luftwaffe* jumped the 390th flying two minutes ahead of us. They got all eight of the low squadron [which was lagging 2,000ft/600m below and behind the rest of the group because of supercharger problems with the leading B-17] in about a three-minute fight. Not fifteen minutes

after that scramble was over about 30 Fw 190s queued up about a half-mile off our right wing. Before they could start in the P-51s hit them. Just before we turned north of Brandenburg they hit the 390th high squadron. I could see the 20mm shells bursting throughout the formation. Four B-17s went down. In the two attacks I saw about 12 fighters go down. Couldn't tell whether they were '51s or '190s."

On April 10, 1945, 2nd Lieutenant William W. Varnedoe Jr., navigator on a B-17 crew in the 385th Bomb Group, wrote: "Immediately after 'Bombs Away', the No. 3 engine was hit and No. 1 was on fire. We started

Above: *Two P-51Bs of the 363rd Fighter Squadron, 357th Fighter Group in formation with B-24J B-24J-160-CO 44-40437 "Hairless Joe" in the 860th Bombardment Squadron, 493rd Bombardment Group.*

Left: *P-51Ds in the 352nd Fighter Group at Bodney escorting Liberators of the 458th Bombardment Group at Horsham St. Faith. Depending on the particular requirements of the Field Order, escort groups would shepherd their assigned bombers for specified periods, taking-over from and being relieved by other fighter groups.*

Right above: *The Type A-10A oxygen mask was prone to icing and uncomfortable to wear and was revised in 1942. By 1943 the A-14 had become standard on high-altitude aircraft.*

Right: *Three P-5ID-5s of the 335th FS and a solitary P-5ID in the 336th FS in formation in August 1944. Leading the formation is Colonel Don Blakeslee and his wingman is Captain Bob Church.*

losing altitude and were falling out of formation, when over the airways we heard bandits being called out by another squadron. A frantic call was sent out on the fighter channel for help and protection from our little friends. And there they came—three beautiful P-51s to help us down and stay with us—one high, one low, with the third dropping his flaps and gear to come alongside and give us the thumbs up and 'V' sign. Then he saw the fire in No.1 engine and up came his flaps and gear and he moved away out. The crew rode it down to friendly territory."

On March 8, 1944, Neill Ullo in the 380th Fighter Squadron, 363rd Fighter Group, celebrated his birthday when the fighters escorted the bombers all the way to Berlin. "My flight and I were attacked by a 109 and I received a shell burst off my left canopy window. I was blinded and the airplane went out of control. I tried a blind spin recovery, felt it go like another spin in the opposite direction, decided to bailout and finally did. I found the canopy release and sensed it blowing away. I was going to release the seat belt and then remove the oxygen mask and throat mike and then jump out of the cockpit toward the extremity of the right wing, as shown in training manual cartoons. But when I released my safety belt I was gone! I found out later that my back was broken from a compressed fracture as I hit the violent air stream.

"Tumbling blind through space, I reached for the rip cord which all through training was near my left shoulder, but it wasn't there. Then I remembered a training session in which they said a pilot had clawed through his leather jacket on the wrong side trying to find the rip cord handle. So I tried the other side but it wasn't there either. Finally I remembered we were using British back-pack chutes and the rip cord was in the center stomach area. I found it, jerked it and handle, cable and all was in my hand. The chute opened and after swinging violently from side to side it settled down and I regained my vision finally. I had started at 28,000ft [8,543m] and I estimate the chute opened about 5,000ft [1,524m]. I landed in the snow as soft as could be. But, when I tried to stand up I found that I could not. I was captured by German troops who saw my descent. They transported me with my broken back to the nearest village jail, then to interrogation and thence to the Herman Göring hospital in Berlin. I was there on my back in bed for three months. I was sent to Frankfurt for solitary and interrogation and eventually to Stalag Luft III."

William E. Kepner, Commander, VIII Fighter Command made the following note: "Complete long-range fighter escort, round trip from England to Berlin, Munich and points east became possible with the addition to the operations of [VIII Fighter] Command in March 1944 of a number of groups of P-51 Mustangs, by large measure longer in range than any other fighter on the battle fronts and superior in many other combat characteristics. The circle was now complete... If it can be said that the P-38s struck the Luftwaffe in its vitals and the Thunderbolt broke its back, the P-51s [gave] the *coup de grace*."

"One Man Air Force"

"Somehow one of our P-51s got separated from his group so he tagged along with us. We were very grateful because he fought as long as his fuel permitted; chasing the enemy until his ammunition was gone... Later we learned his name was Major Howard."

—Lieutenant Joe Wroblewski, a B-17 pilot, 351st Bomb Group, January 11, 1944, when US fighters downed thirty-one enemy fighters, with the P-51Bs representing 8 percent of the escort force, but claiming 51 percent of the kills

Major James H. Howard, ex-Flying Tigers pilot in China, CO of 356th Squadron, 354th Fighter Group, received the Medal of Honor for "conspicuous gallantry and intrepidity above and beyond the call of duty" in action with the enemy near Oschersleben in January 1944, when he came to the rescue of some Fortresses. Howard was flying his usual mount, *Ding Hao!* (Chinese for "very good"). As the P-51s met the bombers in the target area, numerous rocket-firing Bf 110 Zerstöreren attacked the bomber force. The 354th engaged and Howard destroyed one of the 110s, but in the fight lost contact with the rest of his group. He immediately returned to the level of the bomber formation and saw that German fighters were attacking the B-17s in the 401st Bomb Group and that no "Little Friends" were on hand. Howard dived into the formation of more than thirty German fighters and for thirty minutes single-handedly pressed home a series of determined attacks. He shot down three fighters and

probably destroyed and damaged others. Toward the end of his action, Howard continued to fight on with one remaining machine-gun and his fuel supply dangerously low. Major Howard's brave action undoubtedly saved the formation. During the action, he spotted an Me 109:

"I noticed he carried what appeared to be a belly tank. It was a center tank, mounted on the fuselage and not the wings. This was the first Me 109 that I had seen, so I pulled up alongside to make positive identification. I was about 50ft [15m] off to his right and about the same

Right: Major James H. Howard, 356th Squadron CO, in the cockpit of P-51B "Ding Hao!" (Chinese for "very good"). He was awarded the Medal of Honor for "conspicuous gallantry and intrepidity above and beyond the call of duty" in action near Oschersleben in January 1944.

Left: Mustang in the markings of 343rd Fighter Squadron, 55th Fighter Group, P-51D CY-D "Miss Velma" in formation with B-17G Fortress "Liberty Belle" at Duxford.

Below: P-51D 44-11564 OC-W in the 359th Fighter Squadron, 356th Fighter Group, 8th Air Force. The aircraft is standing on PSP matting.

time I saw his markings and determined him to be a 109. He looked in my direction and saw me. He immediately rolled over in a diving turn to the left. I followed him and pulled inside his turn, gave him a burst of approximately 3 seconds. Then he rolled over and went down in a dive. I did not follow him but returned to my position with the bomber. I observed two B-17s go down, evidently hit by flak. One was a direct hit, the effects of which caused the bomber to explode in the air and disintegrate into little pieces. The other one was on fire but stayed in formation for a time."

Flying with the bombers, Howard drove off three Me 109s that were making passes at the formation. Latching onto the tail of one of them, he followed it through the bomber formation and shot it down.

"I was positioned almost dead astern and gave him about four 2 to 3 second bursts, very little deflection. My hits seemed to be in the fuselage center and large clouds of black smoke began to pour out of his ship. I continued to fire until I passed through the smoke. Lieutenant Smith, who was flying my wing, saw pieces fly off the 109 and then the ship exploded. Smith flew right through the debris and his vision was obscured by the oil from the Me 109 covering his windscreen. The Me 109 went into a vertical dive and was last seen going straight down."

The Heat of Battle

Herbert R. Rutland, Jr., of the 360th Fighter Squadron, 356th Fighter Group, would often thank "Mr Rolls and Mr Royce and the Merlin." On his first few missions the Luftwaffe was noticeable by its absence. "At high altitude the sky is a deep purple and completely cloudless. We are at our maximum altitude and in battle formation. As usual, no Jerries are to be seen and I speculate if I will ever get to see one in the air. I remind myself to keep looking around none the less. I scan the sky in all directions and then I happened to glance directly upwards. There, a thousand feet above

Above: The "Donald Duck" P-51D flowen by ace Captain Donald R. Emerson, 336th Fighter Squadron, 4th Fighter Group.

Left: A P-51D Mustang in the colors of Captain Donald R. Emerson's 336th Fighter Squadron, 4th Fighter Group, off the starboard wing of B-17G Fortress "Fuddy Duddy." Emerson was killed by flak on Christmas Day 1944.

us are two of the most beautiful aircraft I have ever seen. Under their sky-blue wings I cannot miss the largest black crosses in the world! My surprise and elation is then jarred by the thought that if these two are above us, then how many more are there pouring down on our squadron?

"In March through April 20, 1945 our mission was escorting B-17s to their targets. Our flight weaves back and forth above the bomber formation. I can see faces peering from the gun ports of the Flying Fortresses. Also, movement of the turrets as the nervous gunners track our Mustangs. The gunners are known to be nervous about approaching fighters, and I hope they identify us as friends. Now smoke appears to be blowing back from some of the bombers. Are they firing on us, I wonder? My headset explodes as someone yells out, 'They're firing at us!' The squadron leader cuts in and says 'Relax! That's just chaff they're dumping out'.

"They don't call Ruhr Valley 'flak alley' for nothing. We are keeping well away from the 'Big Friends,' but within distance to help out if and when needed. Just at this moment there is not much we can do as there are no Jerry fighters because of the flak. The sky ahead of the bombers becomes darkened with bursts, whose black smoke seems to beckon to the oncoming bombers. The 'Forts' plow ahead as though they were aiming for the densest concentration of the black puffs, which now merge with the leading elements of the first squadron. Now the worst is over and the first bombers poke their noses through the murderous flak. Flames emit from two of the bombers, which stubbornly hold their position. One of the bombers falters as flames begin to spread and as we watch several small objects fall from the fuselage. One parachute opens too early and catches alight. To our growing horror the second parachutist suffers the same fate. We are powerless to help and I no longer care to look; all I can do is hope.

"On a high altitude fighter sweep deep into Germany: my altimeter reads over 30,000ft [9,144m] and I have stomach cramps as the gas expands. I am on full oxygen, but a feeling of light-headedness persists. I am cold, very cold, and it seems to be getting colder still. I grope round for the cockpit heater control, which is low beside the seat and out of sight. I don't know if it's set at maximum heating or if I've set it up wrong. I'm shivering and freezing my butt off. Ego prevents me from switching my radio over to seek advice. The first thing I'll do when I get back to Martlesham Heath is to get my crew chief to show me how the damned heater controls work.

"On a mission escorting B-17s to bomb Oranienburg smoke from the smoldering fires of the Nazi capital marked our approach to the target, a few miles to the north. The sky is clear and our 'Big Friends' are in good formation. A few Jerry fighters are reported to be in the area but none came near our sector. As we weave near the bombers they encounter heavy and accurate flak. We move out to the side of one squadron of B-17s. One ship is in trouble and, although trailing smoke and fire, holds steadfastly on course with bomb bay doors fully open. While I watch, I see the flak intensify and assume that we must be close to the target. As we pull ahead of our bombers, our squadron leader starts a turn that will allow us to cross under the bomber stream diagonally. Our flight was now the furthest out and therefore the last to cross below the bombers.

"We were now almost under them, with most of our fighters already on the other side of the stream. I do not like what I see is happening. Our present track will take us directly under the burning B-17 whose load of bombs I expect to be dropped any second. I call out my concern to my

flight leader who at the same time veers to avoid the flaming bomber, whose fate I will never know. Now the radio barks: 'Vortex Yellow, take your flight home... RIGHT NOW!' I've upset our squadron leader by maybe implying that he would expose us to an unnecessary risk! (Later, I am to have my impression confirmed in very simple and direct terms.) Our flight of aircraft has a ball on the way back to our base at Martlesham Heath—a sightseeing tour no less."

"My combat tour lasted just 51 days, during which I completed 20 combat missions over Germany. In that brief time, I accumulated just over one hundred hours—about one third of a tour of duty! I was among the many fighter pilots who felt the satisfaction of having been a part of the final victory in Europe, but whose role was that of journeyman rather than hero. Collectively, we had done the job that Uncle Sam had trained us for. Personally, I had achieved my lifelong dream of flying."

Aces

"No question, the Mustang was a first-class fighter, but its main advantage lay in its fuel-stingy, inline, liquid-cooled, Merlin engine, which allowed it to go all the way into Germany; the same engine presented them with their biggest disadvantage: one bullet hole that compromised the coolant system and that was it—walk."

—Ernie Russell, P-47 pilot, 78th Fighter Group

In World War II the two top-scoring fighter pilots in the ETO and MTO were P-47 Thunderbolt pilots in the 56th Fighter Group. Colonel Francis S. Gabreski was the leading ace with twenty-eight confirmed air-to-air victories and Colonel Robert S. Johnson came second with twenty-seven. Of the top thirty aces in the ETO and MTO, eighteen flew Thunderbolts as well as other types, including the Mustang and Spitfire, while a dozen achieved their scores flying only the Mustang.

The term "ace" originated in World War I for a fighter pilot who had destroyed five or more enemy aircraft in air combat. In World War II neither the RAF nor USAAF officially recognized ace status and its promotion was due principally to the popular press, but the USAAF actively encouraged publicizing the exploits of individual pilots.

The 8th Air Force produced 261 recognized fighter aces. The top P-51 ace was Major George Earl "Ratsy" Preddy, Jr. of the 487th Fighter Squadron, 352nd Fighter Group, who was third overall in the table of aces. He scored three victories in December 1943/January 1944 with the P-47 prior to his unit transitioning to the Mustang. On Christmas Day 1944, Preddy destroyed two Bf 109s near Koblenz and then attacked a low-flying Fw 190, but was in turn shot down and killed by American anti-aircraft fire.

Left: P-51D representing P-51D 44-14151 "Petie 2nd," which in World War II was flown by Lieutenant Colonel John C. Meyer, CO, 487th Fighter Squadron, 352nd Fighter Group, at Bodney.

His final tally was 26.833 confirmed, three "probables," and four damaged.

Lieutenant Colonel John C. Meyer, 21 kills (plus three flying the P-47D), was fourth overall in the table of aces. Captain John J. Voll was the top purely Mustang ace of the war, flying the P-51B and D in the MTO and scoring 21 confirmed kills. Captain Leonard R. "Kit" Carson and Major Glenn T. Eagleston tied on 18.5. Then came Major John B. England of the 357th Fighter Group with 17.5; Captain Ray S. Wetmore of the 359th Fighter Group with 17 (plus 4.25 flying the P-47D); Captain Clarence E. "Bud" Anderson of the 357th Fighter Group, 16.25; and Captain Don Gentile, 15.5 (plus two flying the Spitfire and 4.33 in the P-47D).

Many aces saw combat once again in the Korean War from 1950 to 1953, where F-82 Twin Mustangs shouldered the burden of night-intruder work. The straight-winged F-80C jet fighter should have been no match for the MiG-15, but the battle-hardened American pilots used experience gained in World War II to great effect. During his tour operating with the 4th Fighter Interceptor Wing flying F-86 Sabre jet fighters, Eagleston was credited with destroying two MiG-15s to run his total aerial combat score to 20.5 victories. Major William T. Whisner, who was credited with the destruction of 15.5 enemy aircraft in World War II, racked up another 5.5 victories flying the F-86E.

"Ratsy"

Once he had mastered the P-51, Major George "Ratsy" Preddy of the 487th Fighter Squadron, 352nd Fighter Group, claimed nineteen and three shared kills in just five months. John Meyer said that "George was definitely not obsessed with his score. Many pilots were and would do anything to increase their score. On the mission of August 5, George shot down a Bf 109 which fell into the clouds. He didn't observe the enemy aircraft breaking apart or exploding but merely observed smoke. Therefore, he claimed a probable rather than a kill."

Preddy's greatest day came on August 6, 1944. The night before at the gaming tables in the officers' club, George and his good friend Harry Kidder broke up a crap game. After winning all the money on the table, they started collecting pants and blouses. When he had yelled his final "Cripes A'Mighty!" and made his final roll of the dice, George had won $1,200. He purchased a war bond with the proceeds and mailed it home to his mother.

Missions were not planned the next day because bad weather was predicted so, after the party and several drinks too many, George returned to his quarters and hit the sack. No sooner had he settled down than the officer of the day appeared and announced that there would indeed be a mission. Briefing was in twenty minutes. It was George's turn to lead the group, so he was expected to give the briefing. John Meyer came by George's quarters and saw his predicament. Meyer offered to take the mission. According to Meyer, George said, "No, damn it, I'll take the mission. It's my turn." So Meyer accompanied him to the briefing room.

Normal procedure called for the briefing officer to stand on a platform about the size of a large coffee table while giving his briefing. Normal procedure did not, however, call for the briefing officer to fall off the platform. But that's exactly what happened to George. The group commanding officer looked to Meyer the first time it happened and whispered, "George is drunk!" Meyer said to the officer that it would be several hours before they had to take off and he felt sure that by that time he could get George in condition to fly.

As soon as the briefing was over, Meyer and others made sure George breathed an adequate amount of pure oxygen before takeoff time. **George led the mission to Berlin flying *Cripes A' Mighty 3rd* through high scattered clouds on what turned out to be a beautiful day with excellent visibility. This would be a six-hour mission and since he didn't feel well, George hoped for a milk run.** He recalled:

"We were escorting the lead combat wings of B-17s when 30-plus Me 109s in formation came into the third box from the south. We were a thousand feet above them so I led White Flight in astern of them. I opened fire on one near the rear of the formation from 300 yards [274m] dead astern and got many hits around the cockpit. The enemy aircraft went down inverted and in flames. At this time Lieutenant Doleac became lost while shooting down an Me 109 that had gotten on Lieutenant Heyer's tail.

"Heyer and I continued our attack and I drove up behind another enemy aircraft, getting hits around the wing roots and setting him on fire after a short burst. He went spinning down and the pilot bailed out at 20,000ft [6,096m]. I then saw Heyer on my right shooting down another enemy aircraft. The formation stayed together, taking practically no evasive action,

Above: *George Preddy (right) shakes hands with a fellow ace William Whisner. General John C. Meyer, USAAF, once noted that "I have never met a man of... such intense desire to excel ....George Preddy was the complete fighter pilot." Preddy began his flight training in April 1941, and graduated the following December.*

and tried to go back for an attack on the bombers who were now off to the right. We continued with our attack on the rear end (of the enemy formation) and I fired on another from close range. He went down smoking badly and I saw him begin to fall apart below us.

"At this time four other P-51s came in to help us with the attack. I fired at another 109, causing him to burn after a short burst. He spiraled down to

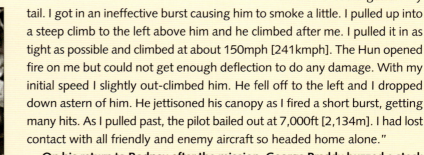

the right in flames. The formation headed down in a left turn keeping itself together in rather close formation. I got a good burst into another one, causing him to burn and spin down.

"The enemy aircraft were down to 5,000ft [1,524m] now and one pulled off to the left. I was all alone with them now so went after this single 109 before he could get on my tail. I got in an ineffective burst causing him to smoke a little. I pulled up into a steep climb to the left above him and he climbed after me. I pulled it in as tight as possible and climbed at about 150mph [241kmph]. The Hun opened fire on me but could not get enough deflection to do any damage. With my initial speed I slightly out-climbed him. He fell off to the left and I dropped down astern of him. He jettisoned his canopy as I fired a short burst, getting many hits. As I pulled past, the pilot bailed out at 7,000ft [2,134m]. I had lost contact with all friendly and enemy aircraft so headed home alone."

On his return to Bodney after the mission, George Preddy buzzed a stack of drop tanks where he knew his assistant crew chief would be snoozing. After he landed half the squadron gathered around *Cripes A' Mighty 3rd* at his hardstand. Word was that he had really put himself into the thick of battle on this mission. George said he would never again fly with a hangover. According to Meyer, George had thrown up last night's party while flying at 32,000ft (9,754m) just before engaging the Me 109s. George's claims for six Bf 109s destroyed were later confirmed.

Three Aces In The Pack

From experience gained in combat Major Glenn T. Eagleston in the 353rd Fighter Squadron, 354th Fighter Group in 9th Fighter Command would break to the right rather than the left if attacked. It was the inclination of fighter pilots to break left and most did. Another lesson was to adopt an "absolute escape maneuver," whipping into a right turn and getting into a whip stall and then snap roll and change the direction of the turn. Eagleston's two cardinal rules were: "Never hang around alone and always send someone home with a cripple," something he himself did on May 8, 1944: "Escorted big friend until 1200 hours and we were in the Nienburg area when four Me 109s came in at six o'clock and 3,000ft [914m] above. I climbed up to engage while my wingman stayed with the bomber. I engaged the last e/a [enemy aircraft], who broke into me and split for the deck. I was attempting to herd off the other three when twelve Fw 190s made a head-on pass at the bomber, scoring many strikes. We attempted to ward off this attack, but it was hopeless. Seven chutes were seen to leave the bomber. The gaggle broke to the right, with the exception of one which made a turn to the left. I attacked the gaggle from astern, firing a two-second burst, scoring hits on the last 190. A minor explosion took place and several pieces flew off. I fired a one-second burst, scoring strikes on the left wing. One and one-half feet of the wingtip disintegrated and the e/a rolled to the left, smoking badly. I followed down and fired another short burst, scoring a few more strikes. He went straight into the ground."

Eagleston's final victory in World War II came on March 25, 1945. He was leading

Left: A set of government-issue playing cards.

a flight in the Frankfurt area once more when two Bf 109s were seen headed for the bridgehead area. Eagleston performed an immediate 180° turn and came in on the six o'clock of one of the Messerschmitt Bf 109s. He fired two short bursts at the enemy fighter and it was enough to convince the Luftwaffe pilot that it was time to leave. This victory made Eagleston the top-scoring ace of the 9th Air Force with 18.5 victories.

In the 8th Air Force General Doolittle's HQ recognized how dangerous ground strafing was, especially when it came to the "aces." VIII Fighter Command also decreed that enemy aircraft destroyed during the strafing of airfields would count equal to air victories in assessing a pilot's score. When, in April 1944, Don Gentile's

Right: Fighter ace 1st Lieutenant Frank A. Cutler with S/Sgt Cy Hall on the wing of P-51B "Gig's Up" in the 486th FS, 352nd FG at Bodney.

score reached thirty victories General Doolittle's headquarters directed Grover Hall, the Debden public relations officer, to delay the announcement. "Seven of Gentile's 30 were destroyed on the ground. At the time there was a burgeoning controversy and confusion over whether parked aircraft should be counted the same as those bagged in aerial combat, though everybody recognized that ground-strafing was far more hazardous than air-fighting. Doolittle's headquarters, whose PRO section was commendably conscientious, did not want to make the distinction between ground and air kills. It wanted to let the newspapers themselves decide how to treat the difference. It was decided that a simple communiqué would be made to the effect that Gentile had destroyed so many in the air and so many on the ground."

On May 19, 1944, Captain Ray S. Wetmore of the 359th Fighter Group, who had four kills flying P-47s, claimed the first of his sixteen victories in Mustangs when he destroyed two Fw 190s. Wetmore scored a triple victory on 27 November 1944 and on 14 January 1945 he claimed four Fw 190s destroyed and one shared destroyed. "In March 1945 Ray Wetmore was under peculiar restraints," his wingman, 1st Lieutenant John F. McAlevey recalled. "He had recently been the subject of a special directive, which prohibited him and certain other top aces from any low-level activity in the combat zone except in the course of actual aerial engagement. The purpose was to scotch the notion that all top aces 'got it' eventually by keeping them away from that impersonal and purely chance hit by ground fire, which can kill an ace as easily as a neophyte and all too often had."

Wetmore's philosophy in combat was to close in to a distance where he still had a reasonable chance of being able to break without colliding. "I always break into the attack. Break to the side and wait for the enemy's next move. It depends on the superior turning speed. In a P-51 that is absolutely your best defensive weapon, you have the best rate of turn. Another hard thing to do but good policy when being attacked—wait until the enemy gets within 1,000 yards [910m], otherwise if you break too soon you will probably be facing a head-on attack."

Left: The G-3 Berger lower-body anti G-suit applied pressure to the upper and lower legs and the abdomen to prevent black-outs during high-powered dives and tight maneuvers.

Above: P-51D "Don Helen" in the 351st FS, 353rd FG.

He also preferred the half roll to the split-S "because during the half roll you can see the enemy a lot better than in a split-S and you do not gain too much speed. I used to see a lot of combat pictures of Germans doing rolls under fire. What good could they be? The P-51 turned its best in a coordinated turn on the verge of stalling, regardless of speed. I would consider a high-speed stall at any altitude above 500ft [152m]. When German fighters go in their pilots usually take evasive action and when they were trying to save their lives they feel nervous and will take a chance where they normally would not. When you start packing a boy's things to send home after he has gone down the more bloodthirsty you get. On the other hand, the more fights you are in I should say possibly the more aggressive you get."

Sorra' Like Sneak Up Behind And Hit Him With A Baseball Bat

John C. Meyer joined the Army Reserves and became a flying cadet, being commissioned a pilot and second lieutenant on July 26, 1940, at Kelly Field. His first assignment was as a flight instructor and he then transferred to the 33rd Pursuit Squadron in Iceland to fly convoy patrols, before returning to the United States to join the 352nd Fighter Group in Massachusetts. He was made commanding officer of the group's 487th Fighter Squadron on December 28, 1942. Meyer became a captain on January 21, 1943, and took the P-47-equipped 487th to Britain that June. The unit commenced combat operations in September, flying a series of bomber escort missions. On November 26, Major Meyer scored his first victory when he downed a Bf 109. During April 1944 the unit began converting to the Mustang and Meyer enjoyed his first success in the North American fighter on April 10. On May 8 he celebrated his promotion to the rank of lieutenant colonel with three victories that gave him ace status.

Below: Major Duane Beeson of the 4th FG, a leading ace, who was shot down by ground fire on April 5, 1944, during a strafing attack and was taken into captivity. He saw out the rest of the war from behind barbed wire at Stalag Luft I, Barth.

Right: John C. Meyer, CO, 487th FS, 352nd FG in the cockpit of P-51D 44-14151 "Petie 2nd" at Bodney. Meyer destroyed twenty-four enemy aircraft in the air as well as thirteen on the ground.

"In every case when attacked by enemy aircraft I have turned into the attack. Since when we are attacked the enemy aircraft has almost always come from above, he has excessive speed and turning inside him is a simple matter. If the enemy aircraft is sighted in time, it is often possible to run into him for a frontal attack. On two occasions I was able to do this and the enemy aircraft was reluctant to trade a head-on pass and break for the deck. Thus I was able to turn a defensive situation into an offensive one.

"The sun is a most effective offensive weapon and the Hun loves to use it. Whenever possible I always try to make all turns into the sun and try never to fly with it at my back. Clouds are very effective for evasive action if there is eight-tenths coverage or better. They're a good way to get home when you're alone. When attacked by far superior numbers, I get the hell out of there using speed, or clouds (there are usually plenty around in this theater) and only as a last resort by diving to the deck. An aggressive act in the initial phases of the attack will very often give you a breather and a head start home.

"The effect of superior numbers in a decision to attack is small. The tactical advantage of position, altitude, sun, and direction of attack are the influencing factors. With these factors in my favor the number of enemy aircraft are irrelevant. It is not wise to attack when the enemy has the advantage of altitude and as long as he maintains it.

"If you're closing fast enough to overshoot, you're closing fast enough to get point blank range. At point blank range you can't miss. I am not a good shot. Few of us are. To make up for this I hold my fire until I have a shot of less than 20 degrees deflection and until I'm within 300 yards [274m]. Good discipline on this score can make up for a great deal. I like to attack at high

speeds and break up into the sun, making the break hard just in case his friend is around. Then I like to get back that precious altitude. We pursue all attacks to conclusion, or whilst a favorable conclusion seems possible. In other words, if by continuing the pursuit it seems reasonable the enemy may be destroyed."

Duane W. Beeson, 4th Fighter Group, scored 17.333 victories; 5.333 of them flying the P-51B in March and April 1944 before he was shot down and taken prisoner of war. "I think that the most important one thing to a fighter pilot is speed! The faster an aircraft is moving when he spots an enemy aircraft, the sooner he will be able to take the bounce and get to the Hun. And it's harder for him to bounce you if you are going fast. Speed is good and should never be lost. When you keep a high speed up you can be sure of closing into range before opening fire, and the closer you get, the better chance you have of hitting him. Also, another good point to remember is that when you are bouncing a Hun you are on the offensive and have the advantage. But things happen in split seconds up there, overshoot him if possible, and hold fire until within range, then shoot and clobber him down to the last instant before breaking away. It's sorra' like sneaking up behind and hitting him with a baseball bat.

"When the enemy is taking violent evasive action it is hard to get a good shot at him if you are going too fast, so speed can be cut down a little just as long as you are still going faster than he is. An attack of this kind prevents the combat turning into a dogfight with both aircraft at the same speed, each fighting for the advantage. If the Hun sees you coming he can turn into you and meet you semi-head on, but you can still zoom back up and-come down on him again. He can't keep turning circles all day; sooner or later he must break for the deck and when he does this, he's had it."

On April 8, 1944, the 4th Fighter Group shot down thirty-one enemy aircraft for the loss of just four Mustangs, as Grover Hall recalled: "How ... to explain the 31-4 battle? The Germans had had every advantage: they were over their own country and they outnumbered the 4th's Mustangs. Without indulging in any alma mater lapse, I submit that the answer is entirely obvious and unquestionable. Simply: the American pilots excelled the German pilots in combat prowess."

Stalag Luft I inmates

The large American contingent at Stalag Luft I, Barth, included Colonel Francis S. "Gabby" Gabreski and other well-known fighter pilots. On March 5, 1944, Colonel Henry R. Spicer, CO of the 357th Fighter Group at Leiston, Suffolk, was shot down and sent to Barth. During a sweep over the Cherbourg Peninsula his P-51 Mustang, *Tony Boy* (named after his young son) was hit by light flak and crashed into the Channel. Spicer was washed ashore after two days and nights in the water, unable to walk or avoid capture. On October 30, 1944, Colonel Hubert "Hub" A. Zemke, CO, 479th Fighter Group, a brilliant fighter leader, with 17.75 confirmed kills in the air, was probably on his last mission before being transferred to a desk job at wing headquarters, but north of Hannover his Mustang was thrown over on its back by violent winds and it entered a dive in which the wing parted from the fuselage. Zemke bailed out before the Mustang disintegrated; he was captured and sent to Barth, where he became the Senior American Officer.

Above top: *German POW Camp (Kriegefangenen) currency.*

Right: *Appel (roll call) at Stalag Luft I, Barth (Ross Greening). The roll call helped the German captors ensure that no-one had made an escape during the night.*

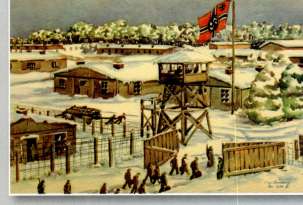

Left: *A snowbound Stalag Luft I, Barth, as depicted by Ross Greening.*

Ground Crew

"One day Staff Sergeant Volie P. Miller, a crew chief, requested permission to speak to me. I was astonished at his request to be relieved from the duties of crew chief, the position being one of the most coveted in the non-commissioned ranks... I was finally able to convince Sergeant Miller that he was in no way responsible for the combat loss of my pilots. It was an emotionally exhausting experience for both of us..."

—Captain Richard E. Turner, 56th Fighter Squadron, 354th Fighter Group

Every fighter pilot knew that his life depended upon the efficiency of his ground crew. They worked long hours, often in appalling weather, to keep the aircraft serviceable and so a pilot should show appreciation and trust in this matter. A tent just off the hardstand was the only shelter that the two mechanics had against the elements.

Out on the line, the mechanics checked the numerous assemblies that made up a fighting aircraft. Putting a shoulder to the prop, a crew chief

upwards. His engine check completed, he chopped the aircraft's throttle and a sudden quiet settled over the whole area, broken by the noise of other planes which, despite their nearness, seemed almost silent. The mechanic left the cockpit and circled the fighter, this time paying particular attention to landing struts and tires. This plane was his, just as much as it was the pilot's who would be sitting in it for six hours today. It must be right.

Above: *An armorer in the 332nd "Red Tails" Fighter Group.*

Right: *A P-51D is hoisted using a crane so that the ground crewman can work on the aircraft.*

pushed it through a few revolutions and then climbed into the cockpit. The engine coughed and spat short flames, then settled down to a gradually increasing, earth-shaking roar. The crew chief kept a close eye on the instrument panel as he checked oil pressure, hydraulic landing flaps, and controls. All the time he eased the throttle forward, holding to the stick as the tail strained

plane's metal bottles. The mechanic wiped off the canopy with a chamois. A last-minute check and pre-flighting was finished. At least one mechanic stuck close to each plane to wait for the pilots, but most of the armament and communications men wandered into their shacks. Rarely would they be called upon this late unless something totally unexpected snafued [Situation Normal, All Fouled Up] at the last minute. They would start a card game and joke about the blonde in town last night, or gripe about KP and other details which plagued them even while the aerial war was at its peak.

Richard E. Turner concludes: "My crew chief, T/Sergeant Clint Thompson of Hatfield, Missouri served with me throughout the war and celebrated every victory scored as if they were my own, which, in a way, they were. For without his unstinting cooperation and long hours of work under the most trying conditions, I could I never have been so successful. In all of my 97 missions, I aborted only one and that was caused by an undetectable particle, in a hydraulic line of an over-age Mustang which prevented me from raising my landing gear."

Above: Corporal Lloyd Shumay directs a crane with a 500lb bomb into place on the wing of a 361st Fighter Group Mustang.

Right: Two armorers at Debden arming a P-51B Mustang.

While the crew chief warmed up the engine, an armorer waited nearby. As soon as the engine died, the armorer opened the gun compartments in each wing and made a quick visual examination of the .50-caliber machine guns, ammunition feed chutes, and bullets. He shook each gun to be sure it was firmly seated in its mounts and would not jar loose while firing. He loaded the guns and closed the compartments and finished his check with a look at the gunsight. As the armorer and the crew chief completed their routine, the men who had eaten early breakfast arrived, and the first workers headed for the powdered eggs. Taking up where the crew chief left off, the assistant crew chief prepared for gasoline and oxygen men who already were servicing planes further down the line. Fuel tanks were filled and oxygen for the high-altitude mission was forced into the

Moonbean McSwine Strikes Again

"As a boy lieutenant," recalled William T. "Bill" Whisner, "I was coerced into giving the name *Princess Elizabeth* to my until-then nameless P-51B by an eager young PIO [Public Information Officer] from New York. Named in honor of 'the' Elizabeth (later to be Queen Elizabeth), it was thought that favorable publicity would accrue to the group should I do some good things in combat in the '51. However, I immediately succumbed to the kidding and changed the name to what I considered the complete social antithesis—*Moonbeam McSwine.*"

Most of Whisner's early combat missions in the 487th Fighter Squadron of the 352nd Fighter Group at Bodney were flown on the wing of Captain George E. Preddy, and he learned much from Preddy, who was to become a top ace in the 8th Air Force and the highest scoring P-51 Mustang ace in the theater.

On November 21, 1944, flying *Moonbean McSwine*, Captain Whisner was credited with five 190s destroyed and two probably destroyed to run his score up to nine and a half aerial victories. Shortly after noon Whisner was part of a composite flight of six Mustangs flying at 25,000ft (7,620m) in the vicinity of Merseburg, Germany. At 12:25 hours fifty-plus enemy fighters were sighted heading toward the last box of bombers that had already left the target. The Mustangs immediately began to climb after them at 29,000ft (8,839m) The enemy fighters were flying twenty-plus in close formation with six three-ship cover flights. As the P-51s approached the enemy aircraft were identified as Focke-Wulf Fw 190s, all of which were carrying drop tanks. Whisner reported:

"Colonel John C. Meyer told me to take a straggler on the starboard and rear of the formation. As I closed on him the formation turned about 45° right and this straggler joined the formation. I fired a short burst at this 190 at about 400 yards [366m], using the K-14 gyroscopic gunsight, but observed no strikes. I closed to 200 yards [183m], fired another burst, which covered him with strikes. Large pieces flew off and he fell into a spin, smoking and burning.

"I closed on another 190 and hit him with a good burst from about 150 yards [136m], knocking pieces off. He fell off to the right and I hit him again with fifteen to twenty degrees of deflection from 100 yards [91m] or

Below: 1st Lieutenant Bill Whisner and his P-51B "Princess Elizabeth" after completing a mission on May 12, 1944. The fighter's unique nickname was inspired by an impending visit by the named royal to Bodney base in May 1944.

Left: *Control stick recovered from the downed "Little Zippie." The "pipper" on top, when pressed, fired the machine guns.*

Left: *On November 21, 1944, Captain William "Bill" Whisner (left) destroyed six Fw 190s and Lieutenant Claude Crenshaw (right) downed five more. With them (center) is George Preddy, who destroyed a single Fw 190 on the same mission to take his total of victories to 24.5.*

Below: *Captain Lt William T. "Bill" Whisner in the 487th Fighter Squadron, 352nd Fighter Group, taxiing P-51D 44-14237 "Moonbeam McSwine" at Bodney.*

less; again pieces came off and he fell into a flat spin. I watched this one go through a haze layer, still spinning and smoking. About this time the enemy seemed to be worried. I saw two of them break off and dive down, taking violent evasive action. I did not attempt to follow them, but stayed behind the formation. I closed up behind a three-ship flight which was flying almost line abreast about fifty yards apart. I put my sight on the leader, but before I opened fire he broke down. I was then almost between the other two. I banked steeply to the right then back to the left and hit the one on the right at less than 100 yards [91m]. Pieces flew off and he fell into a flat spin, smoking and burning. I depended on my wingman, Lieutenant Waldron, to get the one on the left and he didn't fail me. I saw him hit the Fw 190 which went down out of control, smoking.

"I closed on another 190 which was turning from left to right. He saw me and turned steeply to the right. I cut him off and hit him all over in a deflection shot of fifteen to twenty degrees at 200 yards [183m] or less. He went down in a vertical dive, puffing smoke and flame and disappearing into the haze. Next, I saw another Fw 190 going down in flames. My wingman had gotten this one. I made a 180° right turn ... and lost my wingman.

"The main formation of Fw 190s was still intact, but only two ships remained in the cover section. I firewalled everything and caught up fast. I picked the last one, fired at him from 300 yards [274m]. Due to haze and heavy contrails I did not see any strikes on him. He snapped into a tight spin and went down below me. I claim a Fw 190 probably destroyed on this one. I was very close to the main formation by this time. I picked out one of them and started firing from about 200 yards [183m]. He was completely covered with strikes and fell off into a dive. I turned and watched him and he broke into several pieces. I think his belly tank exploded.

"Up to this time not one of the Fw 190s had dropped their belly tanks. I had plenty of time to plan my attacks and those tanks made the 190s extremely vulnerable. As I fired at this last one, the main formation dropped their tanks and dived down and to the left. I followed but lost them in the haze. As I pulled up I saw three of the Fw 190s on my tail so I stood my plane on its tail and lost them. At about 23,000ft [7,010m] I saw a Fw 190 on a P-51's tail. I attacked him and fired a deflection shot from about 100 yards [91m]. As I mushed past his line of flight he flew through my fire. He then leveled off and I hit him from slightly above at fifty yards. My fire hit him in the engine and cockpit; his canopy flew off along with other large pieces. He went straight down with his engine burning and smoking. I joined Colonel Meyer and my wingman and came out with them."

Strafers

"We had P-51 escorts. I watched them dive down and strafe a train.
It blew up as I watched. The train was all that I saw moving on the ground
and soon it did not move. A wood came into view and smoke wafted out
of it; perhaps a sign our fighter planes earlier had paid a call."

—Technical Sergeant Robert T. Marshall, radio operator/gunner in the 385th Bomb Group,
August 11, 1944, mission to Belfort in southern France

On January 1, 1944, the United States Strategic Air Forces (USSTAF) in Europe was established under the command of Lieutenant General Carl Spaatz. "Tooey," as he was nicknamed, could see that the air campaign in Europe would be firmly entwined with the ground campaign in northern France after the Normandy invasion, scheduled for June. First, however, control of the air had to be wrested from the Luftwaffe. Without Allied air superiority Operation *Overlord*—the invasion of the continent—could not succeed. But with the Pointblank Directive three months behind schedule, only by employing long-range fighters offensively in air-to-air combat with the Luftwaffe and in strafing could the timetable for invasion be made good. Spaatz ordered that Mustangs be prised from the 9th Air Force and given to the 8th, while Brigadier General James H. Doolittle, commanding 8th Air Force, put the offensive air plans into operation. "Adolf Galland said that the day we took our fighters off the bombers and put them against the German fighters—that is, went from defensive to offensive— Germany lost the air war... I made that decision and it was my most important decision during World War II. As you can imagine, the bomber crews were upset. The fighter pilots were ecstatic."

Left: P-51Ds of the 354th FS and blue-tailed 357th FS in the 355th FG at Steeple Morden in a tight formation. The small letter "C" on fin or rudder signifies use by command pilots

Doolittle later recalled that, "In air battles during 1944, fighter pilots and bomber crews destroyed over 6,000 enemy aircraft. Strafing attacks by our fighters accounted for 1,950 more. In precision attacks on enemy airfields and factories, our heavies not only blasted production facilities, but also damaged or destroyed an additional 2,630 Nazi aircraft. Fighters also knocked out 3,652 locomotives, 502 freight cars, 3,436 trucks, and significant numbers of tank cars, ammunition dumps, and similar ground targets."

The fighter ace Don Gentile also recalled: "The time finally came for us in late February, 1944. There was no more need to put all our planes in the close support of the bombers. There was no more need to keep the formation at any cost. We were sent out there to go and get and clobber the Nazis. If they wouldn't come up into the air we would go down against their ground guns and shoot them up on the ground. Get them, that was the idea. Kill them, trample them down. It was this time I, personally, was ready for. I had been wanting to fly, and flying was practically my whole life. In the two years of mixing it with the Germans I had learned a great many things that you can't learn in any but the hard way. And there were many in Colonel Don Blakeslee's group who were in the same condition. It was no accident that when the bell finally rang for the big fight Colonel Blakeslee's team became, in seven weeks ... the highest-scoring outfit in the whole league."

Strafing Is A Simple Process

Lieutenant Colonel John C. Meyer, CO, 352nd Fighter Group once observed: "Our group was the first to attempt a penetration in force on the deck for a strafing mission. I do not like the deck. This is especially true in the Pas de Calais area. I believe that it may be used effectively to avoid an area of numerically superior enemy aircraft because of the difficulty in seeing an aircraft on the deck from above. With all-silver aeroplanes, this excuse is even doubtful. The danger from small arms ground fire, especially near the coast, is great. I realize that I differ from some of my contemporaries in this respect, but two-thirds of our squadron losses have been from enemy small arms fire. I led a 12-ship squadron on a 50-mile [80km] penetration of the Pas de Calais area on the deck. We were under fire along the entire route. We lost one pilot, three aeroplanes, and three others damaged. I repeat, I don't like the deck, and can see little advantage in being there."

Frances H. Griswold, Commanding, VIII Fighter Command, noted that: "Since the beginning of this war the profit and loss on the proposition of fighter aircraft attacking ground targets has been the subject of professional debate and pilot discussion. Small profit to shoot up two or three trucks or a couple of machine guns for the loss of a valuable aircraft and pilot. Worse still when two, three, four go down over one well-dispersed enemy airdrome or, as on the days of our large-scale attacks by the whole Command, twenty-five or more may be MIA [missing in action]. In addition to the loss of these planes and pilots is the unfortunate fact that our best, our outstanding leaders and fighters who had yet to meet their match in any enemy they could see, have gone down before the hidden gunfire or light flak incident to a ground attack. Duncan, Beeson, Beckham, Gerald Johnson, Gabreski, Juchheim, Andrew, Hofer, Goodson, Schreiber, Millikan, Carpenter, the list could go on."

Duane Beeson was downed April 5, 1944. 1st Lieutenant Charles D. Carr, who was flying Green #2 to Beeson,

Above: A still from a gun camera in the 78th Fighter Group of Mustangs strafing German aircraft at airfields in the Reich.

Left: Four P-51B and D Mustangs in the 375th Fighter Squadron, 361st Fighter Group, peel off after a sortie on July 11, 1944.

recalled the mission: "We were flying at 8,000ft [2,438m], north of Bordeaux. Beeson called over the R/T that we were going down to strafe an aerodrome. We dove down to the deck about a mile from the A/D [aerodrome]. We approached it at about 400mph [644kmph] IAS [indicated airspeed]. Beeson and

Captain Peters turned to port to attack an Fw 200 on the ground. I was on the inside and I could not turn with them, so I continued to fly straight. I pulled up over a hill and saw what I thought was a Ju 88 in front of a hangar. I fired and saw strikes in front of the e/a [enemy aircraft]. I raised the nose and kept on shooting. Three of my guns stopped at about this time. I did not see any more strikes. I had no reflector sight and was using the mechanical sight. I pulled up over a hangar and continued on for a few hundred yards before pulling up. Beeson called over the R/T saying he had been hit by flak. I looked back and I saw him behind and to the port." Beeson survived and was taken into captivity.

Donald J. M. Blakeslee, P-51 pilot, CO, 4th Fighter Group, used terrain—hills, gullies, and trees—for cover, and such airdrome installations as hangars and the like to screen his approach. "I never come right in on an airdrome if I can help it. If I have planned to attack an airdrome beforehand, I pick an IP [initial point] 10 miles [16km] away—some easily recognizable place. I have my course from there to the drome worked out.

"Once in the air, I take my boys right past the airdrome as if I had no intention of attacking it at all. At my IP I let down and swing back flat on the deck. I usually try to have another check-point on the course from my IP, not far from the airdrome, and when I pass that I know I am definitely coming in on the right field. I don't like to end up on an airdrome before I realize I am even coming to one. But once I hit the drome, I really get down on the deck. I don't mean five feet up; I mean so low the grass is brushing the bottom of the scoop.

"After the attack on the field, stay on the deck for a good mile beyond the drome before pulling up. The break should consist of rudder yawing. Never cock a wing up. If you must turn on the drome, do flat skidding turns. Don't give the Hun a better target to shoot at. I prefer to get down low and shoot up at any aircraft on the ground rather than come in high and shoot down. Usually I fire a short burst from long range and correct for it as I come in.

"In general, my pilots and I realize ground strafing involves a greater risk than shooting Huns down in the air. But it seems to be quite as important. Besides, we get more fun out of strafing ground targets instead of airfields—no one really likes to attack these.

Above: *Colonel Don Blakeslee, who was commanding officer of the 4th Fighter Group, January 1–November 19, 1944.*

"My feeling is that there is entirely too much emphasis placed on methods of strafing and on so-called tactics. Strafing is a simple process. You pick a target and shoot it up. As long as you are comfortable and get away with it, that's all there is to it. Every pilot probably has a different idea on how to do it. A general rule just can't be laid down, for one method is probably no better than another."

Blind Luck

Attacking ground targets cost the American air forces dearly on occasion. John Godfrey of the 4th Fighter Group once wrote that "...the USAAF had issued a directive stating that all German planes destroyed on the ground would be given as credit to a pilot's score. I often think, now, that they were wrong in doing this, for due to strafing, the Air Force lost the cream of its pilots. Skill was not necessary and often blind luck was the principal factor in a successful strafing. The 20mm and 40mm fire of the Germans who were protecting their aerodromes was deadly. Against these insuperable odds we continued at every opportunity to attack the aerodromes. Yet I suppose the risk could be justified at Air Force headquarters; after all, if we could destroy a plane on the ground that would be one less to meet our bombers on the next raid. There was only one fighter pilot's life at stake compared to twelve men in a Fortress. The ruling was like throwing a bone to a pack of hungry dogs. The Air Force threw us the bait and when the German fighters were not in the skies we went down on the ground to look for them."

Above: The 361st FG CO, Colonel Thomas J. J. Christian, in P-51D 44-13410 E2-C "Lou IV IV/Athlene." Christian was shot down and killed during a dive-bombing and strafing mission against rail targets at Arras, France, on August 12, 1944, in this Mustang.

Thomas J. J. Christian, Jr., the only West Point graduate to command a fighter group—the 361st Fighter Group—in the ETO, was not in favor of large "on the deck" missions: "I believe that we should go over at altitude, say 10,000ft [3,048m], pick out a target, drop down so that the formation can follow some definite landmarks to the target, such as rivers or highways, make one pass and then gradually regain altitude. Co-ordinated attacks on one target could be made by flights or sections in this manner. Most groups range or spread out more after a little experience in order to spot and hit the Hun before he attacks the bombers.

Above: P-51D representing P-51D 44-13410 E2-C "Lou IV/Athlene" flown by Colonel Thomas J. J. Christian. Opposite page: Ammo colors. A round of .50-caliber ammunition was 5.47 inches (139mm) long and weighed 1.71 ounces (48g).

"Usually, a successful fighter attack against a ground target requires less skill, more nerve, and as precise an estimate of the situation as an air-to-air attack. We say usually because there are exceptions; for example, successful fighter-bombing is a specialized sport which requires considerable practice and skill; moreover, it does not take any courage to shoot up an undefended target (provided that you know beforehand that the target is undefended); and, it is often much easier to make a proper estimate of a ground situation than it is to make one of an air situation because, in many cases, we are afforded prior knowledge of the target conditions. The latter is never true in air-to-air combat."

Christian was shot down and killed by flak during a dive-bombing and strafing mission against a railroad marshaling yard at Arras, France on August 12 1944.

Joe L. Mason, P-51 pilot, CO, 352nd Fighter Group, had the following to say about strafing: "Shooting up convoys, and especially staff cars and dispatch riders, was considered great sport. On trains and convoys where you encounter no return fire, you must make every bullet count. Our ammunition is belted with five rounds of tracer fifty rounds from the end of the belt. We have a rule that you will not shoot past that tracer on a ground target—we lost some 109s one day

---

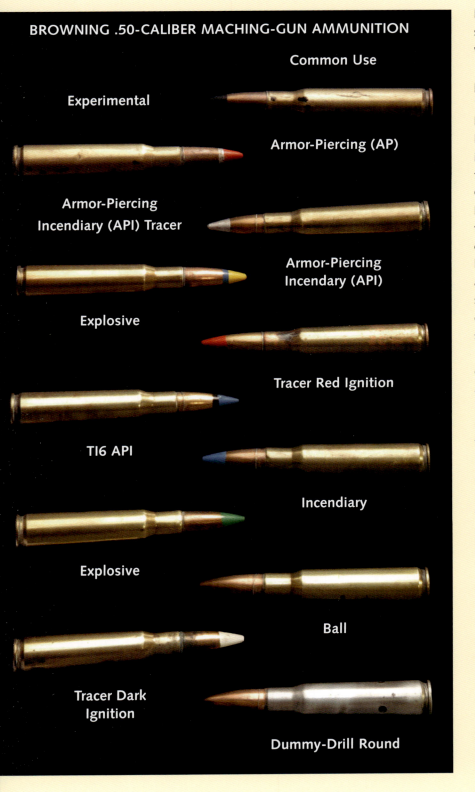

BROWNING .50-CALIBER MACHING-GUN AMMUNITION

Common Use

Experimental

Armor-Piercing (AP)

Armor-Piercing Incendiary (API) Tracer

Armor-Piercing Incendiary (API)

Explosive

Tracer Red Ignition

TI6 API

Incendiary

Explosive

Ball

Tracer Dark Ignition

Dummy-Drill Round

because not a damn soul in the group had any bullets left. And good shooting is good shooting regardless of the target, and good shooting is what kills Germans.

"On specific assigned targets I think bombing with fighters is OK. I'm partial to dive-bombing, as I think it's as accurate as any. Anything less than 1,000lbs [454kg] is not too much good on bridges. On all bridges we've bombed, we have only been successful in dropping one span. I'm sorry to have to admit it, but it seems to be the truth. Bombing with a fighter aircraft is one hundred percent personal skill, and it's just like playing basketball—the more you practice, the more baskets you can sink. We in the VIII Fighter Command have not had the time, ranges, or equipment to practice fighter bombing to even approach the degree which could be obtained. But, we are basically an escort outfit, and, in that, we have had sufficient practice to come closer to perfection. The scoreboard shows that.

MURPHY CARTOONS SKETCHES BY LT. J. L. MURPHY WERE WELL KNOWN ON BASE

"You can mess up a lot of railroad by flying straight and level and dropping one bomb at a time. If done right, one group can break the tracks every quarter-mile for about fifty miles. That should drive the Hun nuts trying to fix it; it's not a permanent injury, but it makes him mad as hell. A good fighter-bomber pilot can hit his target from any dive angle at any altitude; that is what takes practice. A fighter pilot who doesn't want to shoot his guns is no fighter pilot. I continuously have to warn them about non-military targets; the angle they shoot so it won't kill half the French in France, etc."

Avelin P. Tacon, Jr., CO of the 359th Fighter Group, related that: "It is impossible to attack ground targets without having to pull up as the nose of the Mustang rides pretty well down at high speed. If the nose isn't far enough down, you can use 10° of flaps, which is permissible up to 400mph [644kmph]. This will bring your guns down on the ground right in front of you. As for bombing, we much prefer dive-bombing. Skip-bombing is something we are not at all enthusiastic about. Probably because we can't hit a damn thing that way! The only thing we consider a skip-bomb target is a tunnel mouth. All of the bridges we have skip-bombed have had low river banks and our bombs have just tumbled cross-country for about a mile before exploding."

Bounced By Mustangs

"For equal numbers engaged," **said Frances H. Griswold, Commanding, VIII Fighter Command,** "four times as many pilots of this Command are lost on ground attack as in aerial combat. Light flak will ring an A/D [aerodrome] or an M/Y [marshaling yard]. Flak cars will open up in the middle of a train. A truck convoy, with sufficient warning, may be a hornet's nest. Every target of special value to the enemy will be heavily defended and may exact its price. Where then is the profit? The answer is the successful invasion and the victorious battle of France. The answer is our flight of many a heavy bomber mission without challenge by enemy fighters and the presence of our hordes of bombers and fighter-bombers over our troops in Normandy. The roads of France, strewn with enemy wreckage, reply and an enemy starving for oil, ammunition, supplies, reinforcement could answer with deep feeling."

John B. Henry, Jr., in the 339th Fighter Group said that, "Because of the extreme vulnerability of the P-51 airplane to any kind of damage, it is considered by most of our pilots that attacks on ground targets are not worth the risk unless those targets are poorly defended and are extremely vulnerable to 0.50 caliber fire. After a long lull, when no opposition has been encountered from the Luftwaffe in the air, a couple of missions of ground strafing, despite the risk, does a lot for the morale of the pilots. Just to fire their guns and to know they are doing some damage boosts their spirits and tides them over until the next batch of Jerries comes to meet us in the air. Incidentally, most of our airplanes have only four guns and usually at least one or two of them are jammed and useless. One of our 'pet peeves' against this airplane is its lack of fire power in combat models prior to the 'D' series."

Above: P-51D WR-A "Palma" in the 354th FS, 355th FG, which appears to be diving but is in level flight. Occasionally the wings came off a Mustang in a high-speed dive, either from the ammunition bays bulging outwards or the tendency for the undercarriage to extend in flight, both causing abnormal loads on the wing.

On February 3, 1945 Major Leslie W. Seppala in the 353rd Fighter Group was lost whilst strafing rail transportation in his aircraft *Double Trouble*: "The mission was a maximum effort show with 1,000 bombers over Berlin. We escorted the bombers through the bombing of Berlin. After the raid, half the group completed escorting the bombers back to home base in England, the other half stayed over Germany to strafe whatever targets they could find. I found what I thought was a worthwhile target and alerted my four-plane flight. We got set for a strafing run and moved in on a marshaling yard. I fired my guns, but directly over the yard, I felt anti-aircraft hit my plane. I traveled a little distance and noticed my oil pressure drop. I knew I would have to land or parachute. Soon I lost power. I dropped full flaps, kept the wheels up, and landed as slowly as I thought possible onto a clearing near some woods. The plane had a little jolt on landing and it slid a short distance before stopping. I got out and ran to the woods, which were a short distance away. The flight members strafed my plane but it did not burn. I guess they just put a lot of holes in it."

Left: An Fw 190A-7 of 1./JG 1 taxiing in at Dortmund in 1944. In the closing months of the war, due to the Germans' severe shortage of fuel, teams of oxen were used to tow tank wagons and other Luftwaffe rolling stock on operational airfields.

Unteroffizier Walter Ibold, a Bf 109G pilot from the Luftwaffe's Jagdgeschwader (JG) 76 spoke of the experience of coming under a US air attack: "In mid-April 1944, after coming back from a ground-attacking sortie against a large assembly of tanks and lorries near Hof, where the tanks were being refueled at a service station, we suffered an attack on our airfield. There were not only Mustangs, but Lightnings as well. They destroyed nearly all our machines. I lay behind a wall on the southwest side of the airfield beside a transformer station. Behind it stood our NCO armorer with an MG 15 machine gun, firing at the attackers. He hit a Lightning and it went down behind the field.

"The remaining serviceable aircraft in Reinsdorf were moved to Erfurt-Stotternheim. Here we were accommodated in private houses with pleasant hosts. We did a handful of sorties, but without much success. For some days we had visits from a section of two Mustangs who hung about high above the airfield. They destroyed several aircraft during take-off and landing. Frequently a section took off in order to catch the American fighters. One day I took off with a section of four Bf 109s, we flew around at some distance to the airfield, were then directed to the field by radio, placed ourselves up-sun and bounced the Mustangs. Both were heavily hit and went down. The entire section took part in this attack."

"As a protection against bomb splinters and gun fire," recalled Leutnant Karl-Heinz Jeismann, a Fw 190 pilot in the 3rd Staffel of JG 105 at Zeltweg (on the southern edge of the Alps north of Graz) in the winter of 1945, "the aircraft were placed in bays with walls of heaped earth around them. We had problems with ground water and dragging out the machines. Some of the machines were dispersed around the sides of the field under groups of trees. Due to the shortage of fuel the aircraft were not to be moved under their own power but were dragged by teams of oxen. We had 20–25 of them that the local farmer had had to supply.

"On one occasion a farmer and his horse, who were delivering the mid-day meal to working parties around the airfield, became a victim of the bombs. We had removed the 2cm cannon from damaged aircraft, mounted them in twos and threes on home-made turntables, equipped them with sights and batteries and placed them around the field. We had 40 guns all connected by telephone to a central fire-control. The bomber formations arrived regularly between 11 and 12 o'clock, but about an hour before that the fighter escort of 60–100 Mustangs turned up and patrolled the area around our airfield and kept an eye on us. Several times we considered taking off against them, but in view of their superiority in numbers it would have been pointless."

The 8th's Biggest Day

On April 16, 1945, 8th Air Force fighters conducted strafing runs on more than forty enemy landing grounds and installations. The 78th Fighter Group successfully attacked five enemy airfields in Germany and in the Prague-Pilzen area of Czechoslovakia and wreaked havoc, some of the pilots making up to a dozen strafing runs on the airfields. The 78th FG, which was airborne for seven hours, forty minutes, claimed no fewer than 135 enemy aircraft destroyed and a further eighty-nine damaged and was later awarded its second Distinguished Unit Citation for the long mission. In all, the 8th AF fighter groups claimed a record 747 enemy aircraft destroyed for the loss of thirty-four fighters.

BIGGEST DAY DUXFORD PILOTS ESTABLISHED ALL-TIME EIGHTH AIR FORCE RECORD APRIL 16, 1945, BY DESTROYING 135 ENEMY PLANES.

LT. FRANCIS E. HARRINGTON BEARS DOWN ON JU 52, SCORING HITS ALL OVER IT

FW 190 BLOWS UP AS CAPT. DUNCAN M. McDUFFIE, LEADING 83RD, STRAFES IT

LT. RICHARD E. PHANEUF FIRES ON NAZI TRANSPORT AS THREE OTHER PLANES BLAZE

LT. G. B. ELSEY FINISHES OFF PLANE ON CONTROL TOWER'S RIGHT AS LEFT ONE BURNS

OTHER P-51'S ARE PULLING UP (TOP AND LEFT) AS LT. D. J. HENAHAN BORES IN

PLANES ARE BURNING ALL OVER AREA AS LT. G. W. STILWELL MAKES ATTACK

Above: Stills from a gun camera of Mustangs strafing German aircraft at airfields in the Reich on the "Biggest Day" in the history of the 78th Fighter Group.

Horse Trading

"Much as we liked the P-38, we knew what the P-51 'Spam Can' would do and we wanted a piece of the action. For the pilots who had never flown a single-engined fighter before, the conversion was something of a minor trauma. This little beauty had prop torque a plenty and we quickly found it necessary to convert our strong right arms to strong right legs."

—Brigadier General Robin Olds who destroyed five enemy aircraft flying the
P-38, eight more flying the P-51K, and four MiGs in the Korean War

Though transition to the Mustang was easy, many ex-P-38 "Jug" pilots especially were concerned about the suitability of the Mustang for strafing missions. In practice, the versatility of fast, highly maneuverable fighters like the Mustang enabled the Allied air forces to employ them extensively in ground-attack roles, but the vulnerability of liquid-cooled engines to battle damage influenced USAAF policy whereby ground attack was primarily the task of the air-cooled, radial-engined P-47 Thunderbolt. Even so, P-51s of the US 8th, 9th, and 15th Air Forces frequently engaged in ground strafing actions in addition to their usual bomber escort duties. Attacks against airfields often resulted in the destruction of scores of enemy aircraft, but such missions were also particularly dangerous as the small arms defenses were usually formidable. Special procedures were evolved for strafing airfields with the aim of keeping losses to a minimum. Even so, during the course of hostilities, more P-51s were lost to ground fire, than to air combat.

The P-51 was far more maneuverable than the P-47, but pilots missed the solid ruggedness of the Jug. They also missed the smoothness and relative quiet of the P-47. It seemed more frail and vulnerable. One pilot remarked that it was "Sort of like going from a Rolls Royce to an MG sports car." Pilots were sad to lose the rugged P-47, but at the same time realized that the aircraft they were getting was a true thoroughbred. Wayne Blickenstaff in the 353rd Fighter Group compared the two fighters: "As a flying machine, the P-51 was a dream—highly responsive to the controls, fast and extremely maneuverable. Used to the P-47, which had been designed as a high altitude fighter, I was surprised and delighted to discover the P-51 was equally good at altitude. Its in-line engine was noisy, though, which made it seem more vulnerable and less dependable than the P-47 and the beautiful purring sound of its air cooled, radial engine...

Right: P-38 Lightning (top), P-51B Mustang, and a P-47 Thunderbolt in formation. Several groups in the 8th Air Force converted from the P-51 to the P-38 and the P-47 throughout the later stages of World War II.

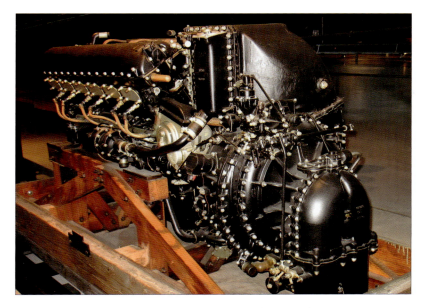

Above: *Packard Merlin V-1650-7-3 engine. Buick's Plant 11, where 234,083 auto engines had been made, turned out its last one on February 3, 1942. Six days later the peacetime equipment began moving out.*

"We knew the P-47 was safe! For months we had watched it return home safely, still flying after incredible battle damage and I wondered about the P-51. Could we depend on it? The Mustang's engine was liquid cooled and it was scary to think that with just one bullet in the coolant line, we'd have had it. However, after putting it through every maneuver I could think of, I was pleased, and had come to the conclusion that the advantages probably offset the disadvantages."

Below: *P-51B "Killer." When pilots were told that they would be changing from the "good old" P-47s that would stand almost any punishment to P-51s, few wanted to change. But they soon changed their minds.*

Flak damage

Though the Mustang was certainly more maneuverable than the much heavier Thunderbolt, most "Jug" pilots considered that the P-51 was nowhere near as resilient to flak damage as the P-47. The Thunderbolt could always be counted on to get its pilot home and many were reluctant to change. Captain Pete Keillor, a pilot in the 84th Squadron, 78th Fighter Group, recalls: "One story on the P-47 concerned a pilot in the 84th before the invasion. He was strafing in France when he ran into a cable. It cut off the bottom four cylinders of the front row on his engine and he made it back across the Channel and crash landed in England. Try that with any other plane. One of our planes that I saw came back with a hole a couple of feet in diameter right at the left wing root. The pilot could have got out of the cockpit and jumped through the hole."

Above: *The 364th Fighter Group, 67th Fighter Wing P-51D 44-14254:5E:G took a direct hit from a 40mm shell in its tail section during a strafing raid on October 24, 1944. Despite wrestling with a jammed rudder for the remainder of the flight, the pilot got the aircraft safely home to Honington in Suffolk.*

"Steeple Morden Strafers"

Claiborne H. Kinnard, Jr., CO, 355th Fighter Group, recalled a mission against a Luftwaffe aerodrome: "Boy, it was better than any movie ever made. Just before we met the bombers, south of the target, fourteen Messerschmitt 109s came streaming along. I wanted to hold the group as intact as possible so we could do the most damage to Ober-whatchacallit, so I told Jonesy to take them. He and his boys knocked down five, got two probables, and damaged one. The rest of the Jerries got out of there. Jonesy and his squadron rejoined us near the target.

"We took the Libs across and went down with the bombs. I streamed across the field once, at about 6,000ft [1,828m], to look it over good and spot the gun emplacements. On the way I planned my runs. Boy, I'm telling you, things looked too good to be true! All the south and east side was literally covered with airplanes, like sitting ducks! A big wall of smoke was rolling up from the hangars, and we used that to screen our approach. Soon as we busted through it, we started shooting.

Above: The official badge of the 355th Fighter Group, with its motto "Our Might Always."

One twin-engined job blazed up in front of me right away. We got to work in earnest. I looked behind me once and, boy, what a sight! I saw two German planes blow up; there was smoke and fire all over; guys pulling up firing, dodging each other, some going up, some diving, and all that smoke and fire. It was the damnedest thing I've ever seen. But there were a couple of surprises coming up.

"I circled the field about the fourth attack and passed over two batteries of heavy guns. It was that high-altitude stuff. I couldn't help but grin, because I could see the gunners just standing there, their heads turned toward the field, with guns too big to use on us. They couldn't depress them enough to hit us. I started to circle once more and all hell broke loose on the field. I looked up and saw a little formation of our bombers going right over us, all but one. He had a wing gone and was spinning down. I thought I'd lost my mind. I reckon they had gotten lost from the main bunch. Luckily, no one was hit badly. We worked a little longer and then the Jerries stopped vibrating and came

Above: The superb 355th Fighter Group memorial at Steeple Morden.

Right: An English Bulldog mascot and his master, Captain James Duffy of the 355th Fighter Group, who was from Mt. Clair, New Jersey, upon the pilot's return to Steeple Morden fighter base following a mission.

out of their holes. They started pouring flak at us like water out of a firehose. We were about out of ammunition, and the place looked like a junkyard anyway, so we started home.

"On the way out, seven Focke-Wulf 190s jumped out of the clouds behind us and started looking mean. I only had four ships with me. The group had split up. We turned suddenly and charged toward them, trying to look just as mean, or meaner. They ran. It was a good thing—I don't know what the hell we'd have done if they hadn't left. We didn't have any ammunition. I sure was proud of those boys. It may take time, but you can't keep those kids from winning. I don't know exactly what it is—but they've got it. One of 'em got a six-inch hole in his wing from a bomb fragment, but they kept right on attacking and came around for more. One even thought that delayed action bombs were going off—but he kept right on going anyway. Maybe that's the answer. Nothing can stop them. They just keep right on going."

The 355th Fighter Group—otherwise known as the "Steeple Morden Strafers"—was cited for extraordinary heroism and outstanding performance of duty in action against the enemy on April 5, 1944. The citation, in part, said:
"On this date, the Group attacked airdromes deep in Germany. In the face of withering fire from ground defenses which increased in intensity with each successive sweep over the airdromes, the 355th Fighter Group tenaciously pressed the attack, wreaking destruction upon parked aircraft and enemy planes attempting to frustrate the attack for forty minutes, strafing not only the primary objective but also adjoining airfields which were in the traffic pattern. Fifty-one enemy aircraft were destroyed, 43 on the ground and eight in the air. In addition 81 aircraft were heavily damaged on the ground and one probably destroyed in the air. This daring assault, carried out in exceptionally adverse weather and against strong opposition, materially contributed to the weakening of the enemy's airborne defenses against heavy bombers."

On April 11, the 352nd Fighter Group provided penetration and withdrawal support for B-17s before breaking away to strafe ground

Left: *A beautiful nude that once adorned the Honor Roll in the 350th FS, 353rd FG hut at Raydon.*

Below: *The original 350th FS, 353rd FG Honor Roll. The nudes are now stored at the IWM, Duxford.*

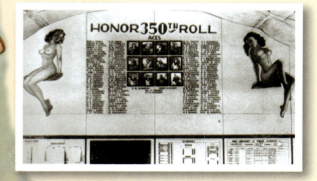

targets. The "Blue Nosed Bastards" claimed three aerial victories, seven more destroyed on the ground, and two Ju 86s probably destroyed and four others damaged.

1st Lieutenant Frank A. Cutler in P-51B *Soldier's Vote* damaged a Ju 52 and got a number of hits on Ju 88s. Seeing a locomotive just leaving the bridge across the Elbe River at Torgau, Cutler made his pass at the engine and saw pieces of it thrown up in the cloud of steam from the boiler. He then flew over the town of Torgau on the rooftops heading west for a mile or two. He shot down a Ju 52 and, as he was on his back heading north and watching the Ju 52 go down, Cutler saw two light blue Fw 190A-7s flying wingtip-to-wingtip directly below, going west at about 1,000ft (305m). Unteroffiziers Heinz Voight and Karl Weiss of 4./JG 26 were flying them.

Cutler headed for them and closed fast, firing on the Fw 190 on the right from about 100 yards (91m). He said, "I saw strikes on the tail section, so I skidded left and fired at the second plane, which had not yet taken any evasive action. All my ammo was gone but the pilot must have been hit since the Focke-Wulf whipped over to the left and exploded in the middle of the field. Then I noticed that the first Fw 190 was burning in the next field a few hundred yards away. I was separated from my flight and the Group, so I climbed to 23,000ft [7,010m] and came home alone."

The Wingmen

"I've been fortunate in that I have always been in a hitting position—leading a flight. It is the wingman who counts. I couldn't shoot down a thing if I were worrying about whether or not I had a wingman. He is the most important guy in the squadron. It is up to the wingman to cover his element leader, no matter what."

—Colonel Walker M. Mahurin, P-47 and P-51D pilot, with 20.75 confirmed air-to-air victories

The basic combat unit was the element made up of two ships, the element leader and his wingman; two elements made up a flight, with the lead element being the flight leader. When they reached the English Channel, the group spread out almost line abreast so that each pilot could cover the other's tail. Major John A. Storch, CO, 364th Fighter Squadron, 357th Fighter Group, has written that "When attacking an enemy aircraft, the leader should go in for the first shot while his wingman drops out and back far enough that he can watch the sky and clear his own and his leader's tail. If the leader overshoots or has to break off his attack, his wingman will be in position to start firing with the leader covering him. If you have to break off combat but want another shot later, break up and either turn to right or left but not in a turn of 360° as you probably will be unable to catch the enemy aircraft after you complete it."

When William D. Wilson in the 352nd Fighter Group flew his first mission on about June 18, 1944, he flew as wingman for Lieutenant Colonel John C. Meyer. "He told me my only job was to stick with him, protect him and back him up. That I accomplished. Close to the target, we encountered a flight of bomb-bearing Ju 88s escorted by Me 109s. The first part of the German formation split-S'ed

Left: Lieutenant John Godfrey and Captain Don Gentile beside P-51B 43-6913 "Shangri-La" in the 336th FS, 4th FG, at Debden in spring 1944, when Godfrey often flew as wingman for Gentile.

through the overcast with the first part of our formation right after them. When we broke through at a very low altitude there were four planes to be seen—Meyer, me, and two planes way ahead of us. I really thought they were P-51s until just before he started firing at them, finishing off one and damaging the second. I finished off the second. We then headed for home, picking up a wounded P-51 to escort back safely. We lost three that day, but accounted for more than 20 of theirs." On the next mission the following day, mechanical difficulties forced Wilson to bail out over France, and he spent the rest of the war in a POW camp.

Captain Don Gentile and Lieutenant John T. Godfrey in the 336th Fighter Squadron, 4th Fighter Group, were legendary for their teamwork. Gentile and Godfrey became famous as "The Two Man Air Force." General Dwight D. Eisenhower went even further, saying to Gentile, "You seem to be a one-man air force." Grover Hall recalled: "AAF headquarters had done all things to discourage the idea of individual performance and to encourage the idea of team-work." Godfrey was credited with 16.333 confirmed victories and 12.666 aircraft destroyed on the ground. On August 24, 1944, Godfrey's Mustang was hit and damaged by machine-gun fire from his wing man, Lieutenant Melvin Dickey, and Godfrey spent the rest of the war as a PoW. Don Gentile's total score stood at 21.8333 destroyed and three damaged.

Wingman's Eyes

Flight Lieutenant Edwin H. King RAF, who was seconded to the 487th Fighter Squadron, 352nd Fighter Group, at Bodney, Norfolk, flew wingman to the 487th Fighter Squadron commander, Major George E. Preddy on the "Ramrod 451" mission of July 17, 1944. "This was my first operational sortie in the P-51D. I flew as number two to George Preddy on 'withdrawal support' for Fortress aircraft that had been bombing marshaling yards at Belfort near the Swiss border. There was quite a large response by the enemy, however, whenever we moved towards aircraft coming within the vicinity of the bombers they rapidly departed, so the sortie was really uneventful. On the latter part of the return flight we had to give close support to a badly damaged Fortress (wing and fuselage damaged and one engine feathered) that was straggling badly, the crew of which fired on us whenever we got a little too close. We saw the Fortress to the UK coast then parted company."

Above: George Preddy's greatest day came on August 6, 1944, when he claimed eight Messerschmitt Bf 109s, though he was later credited with six confirmed victories that day.

Left: Lieutenant F. Stapp and Lieutenant W. Manahan performing a little "hangar flying" in front of "Lady Gwen II."

On many occasions George Preddy would fly as wingman to a pilot in his squadron merely to observe if that man was suitable to become a flight leader. As wingman, he gave up his opportunity to shoot down enemy aircraft because a wingman's job was to protect the man whose wing he was flying on. His CO, John Meyer, had one experience that showed what teamwork could do.

"My wingman and I, attacking a pair of 109s, were in turn attacked by superior numbers of enemy aircraft. In spite of this (the enemy aircraft attacking us were still out of range for effective shooting) we continued our attack, each of us destroying one of the enemy aircraft and then turned into our attackers. Our attackers broke off and regained the tactical advantage of altitude, but during this brief interval we were able to effect our escape

in the clouds. Showing a willingness to fight often discourages the Hun even when he outnumbers us, while on the other hand I have, by immediately breaking for the deck on other occasions, given the Hun a 'shot in the arm', turning his half-hearted attack into an aggressive one.

"Mainly it's my wingman's eyes that I want. One man cannot see enough. When attacked, I want first for him to warn me, then for him to think. Every situation is different and the wingman must have initiative and ability to size up the situation properly and act accordingly. There is no rule of thumb for a wingman. I attempt to attack out of the sun. If the enemy aircraft is surprised, he's duck soup, but time is an important factor and it should not be wasted in securing position. I like to attack quickly and at high speed. This gives the enemy aircraft less time to see you and less time to act. Also, speed can be converted to altitude on the break away. The wingman's primary duty is protection of his element leader.

"It takes the leader's entire attention to destroy an enemy aircraft. If he takes time to cover his own tail, he may find the enemy has 'flown the coop'. Effective gunnery takes maximum mental and physical concentration. The wingman flies directly in trail on the attack. This provides maneuverability, and he is there to follow up the attack if his leader misses. Once, however, the wingman has cleared himself and is certain his element is not under attack, he may move out and take one of the other enemy aircraft under attack if more than one target is available.

"Good wingmen, smart wingmen, are the answer to a leader's prayers. If surprise is not effected

the enemy aircraft generally turns into the attack and dives down, thus causing the attacker to overshoot. When this happens I like to break off the attack and resume the tactical advantage of altitude. Often the enemy aircraft will pull out of his dive and attempt to climb back up. Then another attack can be made. A less experienced enemy pilot will often just break straight down. Then it is possible and often fairly easy, to follow him. Usually on the way down he will kick, skid, and roll his aircraft in violent evasive action for which the only answer is point blank range. Compressibility is a problem which must be taken into consideration when following an enemy aircraft in a dive.

"Eight ships are under orders to remain within supporting distance of each other at all times. These sections operate above, below, around, ahead, behind, and well out to the sides of the main bomber force. The extent of ranging is dependent upon many factors such as weather, number of friendly fighters in the vicinity, and what information we may have as to enemy disposition—the decision on this is left up to the section leaders.

"There is no rule of thumb limitation on who makes bounces. The primary job of the flight leaders is that of seeking out bounces, while that of the other members of the flight is flight protection. If any member of a flight sees a bounce and time permits, he notifies his flight leader and the flight leader leads the engagement. However, if the flight leader is unable to see the enemy, the one who spotted him takes over the lead, or in those cases (of which there are many) when the time element is precious, the man who sees the enemy acts immediately, calling in the bounce as he goes.

"Usually if the combat is of any size or duration, flights become separated. The element of two becoming separated, however, is a cardinal and costly sin. We find it almost impossible for elements to rejoin their squadrons or flights after any prolonged combat. However, there are

generally friendly fighters in the vicinity all with the same intention and we join any of them. A friendly fighter is a friend indeed, no matter what outfit he's from."

Left: Captain Duane Beeson (left), Major Don Gentile (center) and Major James "Goody" Goodson holding all the "Aces" at Debden in March 1944 when they claimed 20.5 victories between them.

Above: A Mustang of the 357th Fighter Squadron, 355th Fighter Group, climbs up beneath a Consolidated B-24 Liberator. During tight maneuvers, the pilot's G-suit inflated to prevent his blood pooling in his lower body. The suit was inflated by the exhaust of the P-51's vacuum system.

Huns All Around

Don Gentile recalled his combat flying in Mustangs in the 4th Fighter Group at Debden during 1944: "To show how a team works even when a big brawl has boiled the team down to two men flying wing on each other, Johnny and I spent twenty minutes over Berlin on March 8th and came out of there with six planes destroyed to our credit. I got a straggler, and Johnny got one, and then I got another one fast. A Hun tried to out-turn me, and this was a mistake on his part. Not only can a Messerschmitt 109 not out-turn a Mustang in the upstairs air, but even if he had succeeded, there was Johnny back from his kill and sitting on my tail waiting to shoot him down. He was waiting, too, to knock down anybody who tried to bounce me off my kill.

"There were Huns all around. Berlin's air was cloudy with them. The gyrations this dying Hun was making forced me to violent action, but Johnny rode right along like a blocking back who could run with the best. After two Huns had blown up and another had bailed out, Johnny and I formed up tight and went against a team of two Messerschmitts. 'I'll take the port one and you take the starboard one,' I told Johnny, and we came in line abreast and in a two-second burst finished off both of them. They were dead before they knew we were there.

"Then a Messerschmitt bounced Johnny. Johnny turned into him and I swung around to run interference for him. The Hun made a tight swing to get on Johnny's tail; saw me and rolled right under me before I could get a shot in. I rolled with him and fastened to his tail, but by that time we were very close to flak coming up from the city. The Hun wasn't so worried about the flak. I was his immediate and more desperate woe, but flak wasn't my idea of cake to eat and I didn't dare go slow in it while the Hun took a chance and put his flaps down to slow to a crawl.

"Then I got strikes on him. Glycol started coming out of him and I had to pass him. But Johnny had fallen into formation right on my wing and he took up

the shooting where I had left off. He put more bullets into the Hun while I was swinging up and around to run interference for him. Then he said his ammunition had run out and I said, 'Okay, I'll finish him' and I followed the Nazi down into the streets, clobbering him until he pulled up and bailed out. The whole thing goes in a series of whooshes. There is no time to

Above: Pilots in the 4th Fighter Group at Debden.

Right: Staffelkapitän Oskar Romm, an Fw 190 pilot who shot down three Liberators in one attack on Sept 27, 1944.

Right: P-51D 44-14923 "See Me Later" in the 335th FS, 4th FG, flown by 2nd Lt Kenneth Green, one of eight Mustangs lost from a force of 743 dispatched on March 3, 1945.

think. If you take time to think, you will not have time to act. There are a number of things your mind is doing while you are fighting—seeing, measuring, guessing, remembering, adding up this and that, and worrying about one thing and another, and taking this into account and that into account, and rejecting this notion and accepting that notion. But it doesn't feel like thinking.

"After the fight is over you can look back on all the things you did and didn't do and see the reason behind each move. But while the fight is on, your mind feels empty and feels as if the flesh of it is sitting in your head, bunched up like muscle and quivering there."

Major John T. Godfrey later wrote: "For this mission Don received the DSC and I was awarded the Silver Star. Of all the stories written about Don and me, this was to be the most widely published. That night the bar mirror said, '13 to 0—Free Beer.' Next day the group destroyed 26 near Bordeaux. Then they revisited Brunswick. Gentile came back with a spirited buzz of the field. As he taxied up, his teeth could be seen through the canopy. 'How many?' Gentile held up three fingers. Then he asked: 'How many did Beeson get today?' 'None'."

Godfrey signed the crew chief's form and walked over to sit on the wing of Gentile's plane. "How'd you get yours, Don?" Gentile was asked.

"I saw a string of them down in a spiral dive and bounced what I thought was the last one in the string," he replied. "I didn't know then that some others were hidden under my left wing. So instead of bouncing the end man, I flew right into the middle of the string. I was a piece of cake for those behind me, but at first they didn't bother me. I got two of the 190s and then found a 109 shooting hell out of me. I got away from him and a little later I got this 109. Godfrey went on down after those that were left in the string. How many did you get, Godfrey?"

"Two," answered Godfrey. "I followed the string down to the deck and started hedge-hopping along behind one. He blew up. Then I got another one. It seemed like I fired for about five minutes. I just sat there cursing him because he wouldn't bail out. But I took one more squirt and his wheels came down and he crashed in some trees."

With the day's triple kill, Gentile had run his score up to twenty-one, swept past Beeson, and stood just one behind Johnson of the Wolfpack. The group total for the day was twenty-four planes destroyed.

Don Gentile remembered that "... after he had run his score of destroyed to thirty, with twenty-three in the air and seven on the ground, we were over Schweinfurt. There were three Messerschmitts just sitting up there in front of me and not noticing me—just presenting themselves as the easiest shots I have had in this war so far. I was positive I was going to get all three. Then I saw a Hun clobbering a Mustang mate of mine. I dropped my easy

Above: *Captain (later Major) Don Gentile. He scored 21.8333 victories in World War II, 16.5 of them while flying the Mustang. He was KIFA on January 28, 1951, at Forestville, Maryland, while flying a T-33A.*

kills and dove on the Hun to bounce him off that Mustang. I didn't think about it at all; it was just a reflex action—nor do I regret having such reflexes. If the feeling for team action had not been developed as a reflex in me—something I and all the other boys can do without thinking—then I would have been dead or a prisoner of war a long time ago."

The More Huns You See
The Easier The Next One Will Be

Colonel Everett W "Stew" Stewart's final tally was 7.833 confirmed destroyed, one probable and four damaged, as well as 1.5 ground kills. Looking back on his career, he recalled: "In individual combat with P-51 aircraft against fighters, it is essential to move in quickly to firing range within the rapid acceleration of the P-51. If an enemy aircraft gets into a good dive before one can get into range, difficulty is usually encountered in closing. The P-51 and Me 109 seem to be about on par for dive and low altitude speed. The P-51 will out-turn the Me 109 at any altitude up to 25,000ft [7,620m] (performance above that altitude is unknown).

"Greater difficulty is encountered in out-turning the Fw 190. I believe that steep, uncoordinated turning is the best evasive action for the P-51 if the enemy aircraft is within firing range. When the turn is then tightened, an average pilot should be able to come into deflection shooting range of enemy aircraft by using a smooth, steep turn. Then, if the enemy aircraft elects to dive away the P-51 should be able to get astern of him. Luckily, I haven't had to use any violent evasive action as yet. If I try something that works, I'll let you know—if not, I'll probably be listed in the mission summary reports.

"In attacking with two ships I like for my wingman to drop back to a position about 250 to 300 yards [229 to 274m] out to either side and about 250 to 300 yards to the rear in such a position where he can completely

Above: P-51B and P-51Ds in the 487th FS, 352nd FG at Bodney, Norfolk, in the fall of 1944. Nearest Mustang is 44-13530 "Millie." The unit introduced a 12-inch (30.5cm) blue cowling band in early April 1944 as its group marking and by month-end this had been extended aft to cover the black anti-dazzle panel too.

cover the two of us from attack. I do not like for the wingman to be trying to shoot one down while I am shooting unless, of course, we are in some so-called 'perfect' set-up. I prefer to give him the next victory and let me cover. My wingmen nearly always get to fire if I fire and they usually come home with a victory. Defensively, I like to have him fly as nearly line abreast as he can maintain. If the enemy aircraft actually attack, we break sharply into the attack and up, if possible. If we can thus get the advantage we can become offensive. If not, we just have to fight. If it is possible to get up into sun, the Hun will usually lose you, or keep going down.

"The four-ship flight is held together just as long as possible, both offensively and defensively. The Hun definitely respects four-ships which will work together, and usually will not attack until he sees he has every other advantage, plus numbers of two or three to one. In attacking with four-ships the flight leader and the element leader move in to fire with the wingmen covering. Wingmen should stay with the leader until both have to split into a life and death dogfight. In flights deep into Germany, wingmen usually get their fighting and firing."

Below: P-51Bs of the 361st Fighter Group's 376th Fighter Squadron taxi out at the start of a mission from Bottisham in early June 1944. All of these aircraft have freshly painted D-Day Invasion stripes on the upper wings and rear fuselage.

1/-

AIRCRAFT
OF U.S. ARMY AIR FORCE

"The wingmen who don't lose their leaders regardless of what they do are the wingmen who win the battle, and the war. When attacked by superior forces, a good offence is the best defense and the best bluff. Other than that just fight like hell. Stay off the deck unless you have business there. Why let everyone and his brother take a shot at you! If the fight goes that low—then good cross-cover with your wingman and flight will bring you back upstairs where you can fight some more. Break off the attack when the German is dead, or the question arises as to whether you and your flight can get home or not. Faith in yourself and your ability to kill a German will give you the determination to press your attack to a successful conclusion.

Above: *Aircraft of the US Army Air Force booklet.*

Right: *Fw 190A-7 Wk-Nr. 340283 of 3./JG 1 is refuelled at Dortmund in January 1944. This aircraft was lost in combat on February 8, 1944, the pilot perishing when the fighter crashed near Charleville.*

Ace pilot Colonel Joe Lennard Mason, CO 352nd Fighter Group, explained the tactical principles of the wingman: "We operate a basic formation of an eight-ship section—two flights, with one flight covering the other at all times. I firmly believe that this eight-ship section can fight any number of Huns at any altitude at any place—provided that it flies it correctly—each man doing his part. It is impossible for a formation to get bounced before it's too late to do anything about it if everyone is doing his job. This is based on the theory of cross-cover—line abreast or nearly so. The same principle holds good whether it's a two-ship formation or a 200-ship formation. He who hesitates is lost. This goes if it's a bounce or if you are the one that is bounced. I would at this point have killed more Germans if I had not hesitated so long on my bounces. The more Huns you see the easier the next one will be. And the same goes for the kills; each one gets easier than the last.

"The bomber support itself depends on how many fighters you have to cover a certain number of bombers. The greater the fighter depth the better the support. Depth in this case meaning the amount of sky in all directions from the bombers that you can saturate with fighters. You must look at the situation upon rendezvous and place your forces accordingly where they will do the most good. The group leader must know at all times where all parts of his group are. Use the bomber formation as a reference point in putting your group back together after combat or escort. If the ground can be seen, then that can be used too. On pulling out, enough strength should be put together to offer mutual support. The Hun will hesitate to bounce a unit which looks like it knows what is going on, and has sufficient numbers to repel an attack.

Down In The Drink

**"All went well until we were about three miles from the English coast.
Then my coolant valve let go and dumped my engine coolant. It immediately
'showed' an engine overheat and was on fire. It quit dead."**

– Captain Huie Lamb, 78th Fighter Group

On December 29, 1944, thirty P-51Ds in the 78th Fighter Group at Duxford escorted the "Big Friends" who attacked the Frankfurt and Aschaffenburg railroad marshaling yards. Among those making their way home were Captain Huie Lamb and his wingman, Flight Officer John C. Childs. Huie Lamb had flown forty-five missions on P-47s and this was his first mission in a P-51, which he had named *Etta Jeanne,* for his younger sister. Huie Lamb recalls the drama that unfolded off Orfordness on the Suffolk coast.

"In the target area we had just made rendezvous when Childs pulled in close and pointed to his headset—a signal that his radio was acting up. I got

Rudder pedal recovered from a P-51 which crashed in the North Sea.

on his wing and after calling our leader we headed for home. No radio called for an immediate abort. All went well until we were about three miles [5km] from the English coast. Then my coolant valve let go and dumped my engine coolant. It immediately 'showed' an engine overheat and was on fire. It quit dead. With the fire and dead stick, I knew I had to get out fast. I tried to open the canopy and then to jettison it. It was jammed. I had already unsnapped my seat belt and pulled off my shoulder harness, expecting to get out PDQ... Maybe I could make it to shore as I could see it quite plainly. At least I would not die of drowning, trapped in the cockpit of my plane but I was falling too fast and could see I was going to hit way short and in the water. What happened next, I cannot exactly remember.

"I came to, thrashing about in the water. I was free of the cockpit, as the canopy had apparently jarred loose when I hit the water. Dazed from the impact and hitting the gun sight with my face, the cold seawater must have revived me enough to kick free of the plane. It sank in no more than 5–6 seconds. Had I not loosened my belt and harness, I'd have gone down with the plane. Normally I'd have left everything fastened, had I intended to ditch. Talk about a miracle. I grabbed for my dinghy and inflated it." Fortunately, Childs had transmitted a "fix" on Lamb's position and then guided a Walrus Air-Sea Rescue (ASR) aircraft to the position. "With only a

Left: An RAF Air-Sea Rescue Westland Walrus amphibian of the type used to rescue Captain Huie Lamb off Orfordness on December 29, 1944.

Right:
Emergency light from a "Mae West life preserver (so named by the RAF pilots after the famous Hollywood movie actress).

Above: Winged goldfish on the sleeve of the "Ike" Jacket worn by James E. Frolking of Cleveland, Ohio, a 479th FG pilot based at Wattisham, Suffolk, who bailed out of a P-51D over Holland on October 7, 1944. Frolking finally made it back to his home base on November 4, 1944 to become a member of the famous "Goldfish Club."

speed of a little over 85mph [134kmph], John had to constantly circle, gradually leading them back to where I was bobbing like a cork and clutching my dinghy. I didn't have the strength to climb inside.

"The Walrus easily set down on the 10 foot swells, in near perfect weather conditions—a rare day on the North Sea. They maneuvered alongside and their swarthy radio operator reached out and literally plucked me from the water. I hung to my dinghy, so tight that at first he could not lift me out of the water. Then realizing I could not help any, I let go of the dinghy. Once inside the rear hatch doorway, they offered me no medication or first aid of any kind. It would be only 10–15 minutes and we'd be back to Martlesham Heath, shared with the British ASR. Then the Walrus refused to start. Finally after the sixth attempt it started and we were airborne and headed inland.."

Little Zippie

At 09:30 hours the 436th Fighter Squadron took-off from Wattisham into the gray cold clouds. Led by Captain C. P. Duffie, they rendezvoused with the "Big Friends" near the coast.

Once their mission was complete, they turned for home, but one of the P-51s developed engine trouble. *Little Zippie*, piloted by 22-year-old Flight Officer Raymond Earl King (pictured), was detailed to escort the crippled Mustang over the North Sea and home. It was only King's seventh combat mission, having arrived in England as a replacement pilot in November 1944. As King and his partner slowly edged across the cold unforgiving water, *Little Zippie*'s engine started to sound very rough. They were no more than minutes

away from the Clacton coastline when the engine gave its last gasps of life. Ray had pushed the throttle wide open in an effort to keep her going, but the prop blades came to a silent halt. At 14:42 hours the P-51, splashed down, making a perfect ditching. Ray had slid open the canopy and didn't even bother to release the life-raft. As he climbed out, and jumped into the water, the sudden icy chill almost held him in a vice-like grip. Meanwhile, overhead Lieutenant Zellmum had circled overhead constantly reporting his position until he was ordered to set a course for home. Two air-sea rescue aircraft were scrambled, as well as the Clacton Life Boat, whose crew had actually witnessed the Mustang's demise. At 15:10 hours, Ray's limp and frozen body was hauled over the edge of the life boat. The crew hugged him very close to their bodies to try and get some warmth into the young pilot. As they sped for shore, Ray's life ebbed away and *Little Zippie* turned upside-down and sank to the sea-bed. King died at Clacton Hospital on January 13, 1945. After the war, the wreck of the aircraft was recovered (picture here) and is today displayed in the East Essex Aviation Museum.

Encounter at Remagen

Captain Ray S. Wetmore of the 359th Fighter Group explained something of the challenge of being a new wingman: "The new pilot going out on my wing has only one requirement I ask of him. That is, 'Do not lose me'. I figure on his first mission I can keep both our tails clear. As he becomes more accustomed to combat I expect more, but on his first few missions I don't even expect him to shoot at Germans. I do not at any time want anyone on my tail. I ask them to stay as far abreast as possible. When I go into attack I go in full throttle. Sometimes it is awfully hard for the men to keep up. The further behind the wingman falls, the further out he must fly so I can still see him. After the first few missions if an enemy plane comes in on my tail and the wingman does not warn me I shall probably tell him about it when he gets back. After all, that is his job."

Above: *Two M1940 stainless steel identification tags or "Dog Tags," made by Sweet Manufacturing Co., were issued to every US soldier and airman.*

John F. McAlevey flew as Wetmore's wingman on March 10, 1945, when the group's three squadrons escorted a small force of B-17s on a bombing mission over the Ruhr. "Halfway back in the 370th Squadron formation Captain Wetmore, the top ranking US fighter ace in the ETO, was leading his flight of four ships. He had recently been the subject of a special directive, which prohibited him and certain other top aces from any low-level activity in the combat zone except in the course of actual aerial engagement. If Wetmore was supposed to leave when the group began its descent that day, he did not. The temptation was too great. We were being vectored to Germans no one could see from above, not even Wetmore who was credited with 'X-ray eyes' by the other pilots.

"Wetmore was hard on his wingmen. He was a quick, wordless, and erratic mover. An instinctive hunter, the few times he led the squadron he managed to scatter it all over the sky. His wingmen were often left far behind also. This was only my 10th mission, but I had now flown as his wingman several times. He couldn't lose me and I became his regular wingman for the rest of the war.

Above: *P-51D-15-NA Mustangs "Develess 3rd" and 44-15016 "Heat Wave" of the 369th FS, 359th FG, 67th Fighter Wing at East Wretham.*

Left: *Captain (later Major) Ray S. Wetmore in the 370th FS, 359th FG who destroyed 21.25 enemy aircraft, February 1944–March 1945, flying P-47s and P-51B/Ds.*

"I stayed with him now in the maneuver in the clouds. The leader of the flight behind, having no forewarning of the course change, was not prepared to follow and consequently lost visual contact with us. The following flights continued to descend on the original group heading, a course chosen by the colonel to break through the overcast upstream of the bridge. The group would then turn north and fly down the river in the clear looking for Jerries. All, that is, except Wetmore and me. Wetmore's course change early in the descent put him miles north of the group. We were unwittingly descending on a course, which broke us out right over the bridgehead at Remagen. I was startled to see flames erupt from the underside of Wetmore's ship. I was only inches away from Wetmore when he was hit. Still engrossed in his instruments, Wetmore did not know he was on fire. The thumping of the hits in the clouds with no visual evidence of flak could be indistinguishable from turbulence.

"When I radioed that he was on fire, Wetmore took one fast look out of the cockpit and then back to the instruments—we were dangerously low now and loss of control could be death by spiraling out the bottom with no room for recovery, but at almost that instant we broke out. Now Wetmore eluded his new wingman for the first and last time. Still saying nothing, he decided this flak-filled area at low altitude in the hills over a river was no place to bail out. All alone with no function to perform and the sole target of every gun, I decided to get out of there.

"Wetmore was calling for help. His canopy had jammed. Wetmore was paying a second price for his keen vision and alertness. He was the darling of our group's intelligence officers. Many times at debriefing he reported seeing things of significance on the ground which others had not seen. A special camera had therefore been fitted to the back of his armor plate and aimed off one of the wing tips so he could bring home photos for S-2 if he thought the subject worth recording. The cross support for the bubble canopy of the P-51 was right behind the pilot's armor plate when closed. Bubble canopies are normally closed when jettisoned. But the one in Wetmore's plane needed to be rolled partly open first because of the camera. No one had warned him of that. The canopy when released had

Above: *Bendix Aviation Corporation Baltimore MD, Signal Corps Radio frequency Control Box BC-602-A. The VHF Command Radio SCR-522-A, based on the British TR1143, was the principal operational set for verbal communications with both 8th Air Force bombers and fighters.*

snapped into the slipstream only to ram its cross-arm into the bottom side of the camera, thus seizing the bubble securely so that it could move no further. Trapped in a plane set afire by our own anti-aircraft, the man who had been prohibited from strafing in order to spare him this very fate was now calling for a homing to a field, any friendly field where he could put down.

"Back at the pilot's quarters, I learned the score. No Germans racked up, but three of our ships and two pilots lost. Wetmore was safe. The fire had burned out before he reached the second field and, with his hydraulic system shot out, he bellied in safely without wheels or flaps... Wetmore was the highest scoring Yank pilot on duty in the ETO at the end of World War II. Twenty-one victories in the air and 3½ ground kills were officially his. As his wingman, I can testify that he never again ventured below 10,000ft [3,2808m] over the continent except in hot pursuit."

Below: *Three Mustangs of the 359th Fighter Group at East Wretham, Norfolk. A new P-51D, 44-13669 CV-I "Pegelin" in the 368th Squadron, which accompanies two P-51Bs from the same unit, has yet to receive its fin fillet.*

On The Deck

"On June 10 we escorted another paratroop drop behind Utah Beach. It was an uneventful mission for us since the German aircraft were still nowhere to be seen. On our return flight we utilized the range of our Mustangs to roam deep behind the beachhead to shoot at railroads, roads, supply dumps, or whatever we could find..."

—Captain Richard E. Turner, *Short Fuse Sallee*, 356th Fighter Squadron, 354th Fighter Group

The IX Air Support Command was activated on December 4, 1943, and on re-designation to IX Tactical Air Command (TAC) on April 4, 1944, took control of four fighter wings, the 70th, 71st, 84th and 100th, from IX Fighter Command. During the spring of 1944 most of the Fighter Groups in IX TAC moved to the Advanced Landing Grounds (ALGs) of southern England, to be closer to the south coast and thus to enemy-held France. The eleven fighter groups controlled by IX TAC were now located on airstrips mainly in the Hampshire area, some of them airfields of a more permanent nature, while the XIX TAC's seven groups were all at ALGs in Kent or Sussex.

As D-Day neared, the 9th Air Force was given the responsibility for destroying all major road and rail bridges in northern France. On June 13, the 354th Fighter Group was informed that it would soon move across the Channel to an advanced fighter strip on the beachhead, in order to give close support to the army advance. Thus its work with the 8th Air Force came to its conclusion. Operations continued under the XIX TAC of Brigadier General Otto P. Weyland.

The success of the concentrated "softening-up" process soon became obvious, as the Luftwaffe was unable to oppose the cross-Channel landing to any great effect. The 9th prevented the rapid movement of German forces, thus allowing the Allies to secure firm positions, and overwhelming mastery of the air, enabling Allied ground forces to move forward with much more freedom. As soon as airstrips built in Normandy by IX Engineer Command were ready, IX TAC Groups began to move to them. Just after D-Day, IX TAC headquarters was moved to France and, by the end of June 1944, five of its fighter-bomber groups were fully operational, attacking enemy airfields, roads, railways, and supply dumps in France, Belgium, and Holland.

A second Distinguished Unit Citation was received by the 354th for its fighter sweeps on August 25, 1944, when group aircraft battled with twenty-five or more Fw 190s in the Reims area, shooting down ten of them and destroying several on the ground. On September 4, the 363rd Fighter Group was redesignated as the 363rd Tactical Reconnaissance Group in order to take on a new role.

The 370th Fighter Group converted to Mustangs in February 1945. The 67th Tactical Reconnaissance Group was equipped with the F-6B and the seven squadrons it operated at one time or another carried out low-level photographic sorties along the French coast, before employing their expertise in support of the landings on June 6. The 10th Photographic Group also operated the F-6B, as well as various other types.

Left: Flying in tandem with a Spitfire, a Royal Canadian Air Force (RCAF) P-51D. Beautifully restored, the aircraft is painted in the markings of RCAF 442 Squadron .

"Ole Dick"

The 354th Fighter Group flew a fighter sweep of Luftwaffe airfields in Châteauroux, Conches, Chartres, and Bourges on April 5, 1944. At a point central to the targets the group separated and Captain (later Major) Richard E. Turner led his squadron in *Short Fuse Sallee* **to hit Bourges airfield.**

"Twenty miles [32km] from target I instructed Green flight to fly over Bourges at 10,000ft [3,048m] as top cover and deployed Red, White, and Blue flights on courses at deck level so they could hit from three different directions at one-minute intervals. I hit the field first with Red flight and caught a landing Me 410, hitting him on the landing roll and causing him to burst into flames leaving a trail of debris down the runway.

"Banking around after my first pass, I dived on a Me 110 being serviced on a hardstand, starting a raging fire beneath him as my incendiaries and those of my wingman ignited the gasoline spilling from the tanks. Pulling up again, I rolled over and down on another twin-engined craft poised at the edge of the field with props revving for take-off. The burst from my 50s chewed into him at perfect range and he blew up.

"Calling the squadron, I told everyone to climb to 15,000ft [4,572m] and rendezvous ten miles [16km] northwest of Bourges. The Germans' surprise had worn off and flak reaction was coming hot and heavy. Everyone except Goodnight got away safe. As he attempted one last pass on a camouflaged fighter at the edge of the airfield, he was hit with a 20mm right below his cockpit. Goodnight thought he could still fly it, so I told him to come on home with us. With Bob fuming over the RT about 'hardhearted squadron commanders' we made our way home, unhindered by the Germans except for an occasional heavy flak burst. Back at base we found one of the other squadrons wasn't so lucky and had lost a fighter and pilot to flak while strafing. But the group had destroyed six enemy aircraft, with one probable and four damaged. We were all convinced of one thing: that was that it was a lot more difficult to attack German aircraft on the ground than in a nice uncomplicated air fight."

After escorting the glider "trains" on D-Day, the 354th Fighter Group had then set about wiping out strategic targets near the front line, as Richard E. Turner recalled: "On the 12th of June we set up a concentrated

Above: What a P-51 might use up in a day of around-the-clock duties as bomber escort. Drop tanks enabled the aircraft to stay aloft for more than nine hours.

attack on a railway bridge near Rouen and plastered the bridge, but good! After the attack I flew back over it alone to check results after the smoke and debris had cleared. We had hit it with 32 500-pounders and most of them must have scored well, for at both ends the tracks ended with twisted stubs with the intervening bridge crumpled into the canyon below.

"Turning northeast I decided to take the squadron around the countryside for a little predatory hunting. There had been reports received of enemy aircraft in this general area of France and I felt that a look-see couldn't hurt. Within fifteen minutes I heard someone in the squadron exclaim excitedly over the RT, 'There's a great big pasture down there at three o'clock with a whole flock of Fw 190s tailed into the hedgerows!' Stabbing my eyes downward to the right, sure enough, there was a large field and parked fighters poked their tails in scattered groups out of the foliage of the hedgerows.

"Quickly checking the area I couldn't see any flak positions so I called to the squadron to follow me and rolled over into a dive. As the nearest line of five Fw 190s crept into range I fired off long bursts and slowly let my fire walk through them as I bore down upon them. Before long two had caught fire and were

Below: P-51B A9-V 42-106485 "Maggie's Drawers" in the 380th Fighter Squadron, 363rd Fighter Group, heads out on a mission.

Top right: *Mustangs in the 380th FS, 363rd FG, 9th Air Force peel off in preparation for landing at Maupertus, their forward airfield in France.*

Lower right: *A 9th Air Force Mustang photo-reconnaissance aircraft warms up in France for a reconnaissance mission.*

obscuring the others, billowing smoke. I pulled upward from the deck in a shallow turning climb to the left and saw ahead of me, alongside another hedgerow, a single Fw 190 being refueled from a truck. Rolling out level and depressing the nose of the Mustang I let fly with another hard burst of .50s. Within seconds the truck exploded in a brilliant flash, engulfing the hapless aircraft.

"Pulling up again I observed that my team had established an orbital traffic pattern around the perimeter of the field. They looked like a circle of Yo-yos as they bobbed up and down, taking shots at targets of opportunity.... As I passed at 1,500ft [475m] I saw a dust trail in another field ten hedgerows away. Calling to my squadron to break off their strafing for assembly at 10,000ft [3,048m], I headed in a shallow dive for the dust cloud ahead. I discovered the dust came from a Ju 88 on its take-off run. He probably saw me coming, because he set his plane back on the ground. I hit him just as he rolled to a stop and he exploded. With our ammo practically expended and signs of a hornet's nest being stirred up by our activities, it was time for 'Ole Dick' and my boys to hit the trail for home. Safe back at base ... we sorted out the results. Besides the bridge, the squadron reported a count of twenty burning Fw 190s and with my bonus Ju 88, the total destroyed ran to twenty-one."

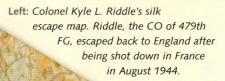

Left: *Colonel Kyle L. Riddle's silk escape map. Riddle, the CO of 479th FG, escaped back to England after being shot down in France in August 1944.*

Air Defense—The Country Cousin Of Air Offense

The 363rd Fighter Group had arrived in England at Christmas 1943, fresh from training in California. P-51 aircraft were received in January 1944 and the group's first operation was mounted on February 23. For the next four months the group escorted bombers and fighter-bombers to their targets in France, Germany, Belgium, and Holland, and also strafed strategic targets. Elmer W. O'Dell, one of the 363rd Fighter Group's pilots, recalled: "I destroyed an aircraft on my first mission. Unfortunately, it was a P-51. I was taking off on my leader's wing when I blew a tire and swerved toward him. Kicking opposite rudder, I avoided the collision, but by the time I got straightened out I didn't have enough speed or runway to get airborne. I cut the switches, held the stick in my gut, and closed my eyes. The plane ran off the field, across the sunken road which sheared off the gear, dropped on two full wing tanks, skidded across a field, tore off the left wing on a stump, and wound up with its nose in a chicken coop. I was told later that I killed a crow in a hedge along the road and two chickens in the coop. The Mustang was rugged. I didn't even get a scratch."

Lieutenant Colonel James B. Tipton commanding the 363rd Fighter Group explained operations over the Normandy beaches: "The invasion vehicles and beachhead must be preserved from crippling air attacks at all costs. This called for air defense, pure and simple, the country cousin of air offense but an essential element of the air superiority battle none the less. The 354th Group became the hunter, ranging far in advance and seeking the enemy before he could attack. We became the watchdog, the reserve in the rear to fend against wolves who might slip through the forward screen.

"For the most part, our role consisted of monotonous patrols over the crowded sea routes crossing the Channel and over the beachheads. Later, when XIX TAC moved to Normandy, the 363rd was established at an airfield closest to the Channel from whence we continued air defense, surveillance of our forces on the Continent and the shipping which supplied them with men and munitions. The relative experience and records of the two P-51 groups made any other arrangement illogical."

On D-Day—June 6, 1944—the 363rd Fighter Group escorted IX Troop Carrier Command (TCC) C-47s towing CG-4 gliders over Normandy and attacked frontline positions. Lieutenant Ed Kemmerer flew his last flight in the 381st Fighter Squadron, 363rd Fighter Group, on June 17, 1944 when he was one of eighteen pilots on a dive-

Below: Glenn Eagleston in his Mustang. On February 10, 1944, on a mission to Brunswick, his Mustang was damaged by flak but he managed to get it back to England before bailing out. Eagleston was the top-scoring ace of the 9th Air Force.

bombing **"show"** attacking **locomotives, rail cars, and a bridge near St Lô.** "The weather was not as expected, low cloud cover. So we were flying at about 2,000ft [609m], just under the clouds, when I got hit and a terrific heat came into the cockpit. Not wanting to burn, I bailed out immediately. Fortunately, I had just enough altitude for the chute to open. I landed flat on my back and was knocked 'silly.' While getting out of my parachute harness something stung me in my leg the same time I heard the gun shot. They must have yelled at me before the 'warning shot' but with the noise and confusion and my unawareness I didn't hear them. The warning shot nicked my shin, barely drawing blood. I was very happy to be alive. So after sharing my cigarettes and getting a little first aid they took me to their HQs and I started my journey to Stalag Luft III at Sagan, Germany."

On June 16, Lieutenant Colonel (later Brigadier General) "Tommy" L. Hayes, Jr., an 8.5-victory ace, led the 357th Fighter Group on a strafing mission against two trains in southern France. Colonel Hayes recalled: "Nothing was observed except a marshaling yard at St. Pierre,

Left and below: An 85 US gallon (322-liter) P-51 fuselage tank (pictured with a close-up of the fuel gauge), internally positioned behind the pilot's cockpit.

30 miles [48km] south of Poitiers, with three lines of goods cars and other stray cars totaling one hundred cars in all. About one mile north, a train of thirty goods cars was rather neatly camouflaged by being parked between a cut of trees on a sharp bend. We flew south of Angoulême and observed congested traffic, but I returned to St. Pierre as it looked like it was safe from flak. Having two squadrons now seemed to work smoothly and not too congested. The 363rd Squadron was raising hell at Poitiers at this time.

"Flying north on the sun side I left the 362nd at 9,000ft [2,743m] as top cover. I made a diving turn, slipping through some cloud at 3,000ft [914m] and ended up on the deck, approaching the yard from the west or 90° to it. My flight of four was slightly staggered abreast and coming in at 400mph [644kmph], all firing ahead. As each one reached the cars, he released his tanks which sprayed the gasoline around. The second flight, not far behind, fired into the burst tanks, setting many of the cars on fire; and then in turn released their tanks as they passed over. My second section of eight Mustangs at this time splashed their tanks on the thirty cars one mile north...

"We all made one pass, strafing to increase damage and fire. Then we pulled up to cover the 362nd while they got in on the fun. This second squadron picked out sections of cars and buildings still not burning. There was no use in strafing any more as the fires spread quickly. It was now that ... two flak cars started to fire, one on each side of the middle train. One element gave him two gas tanks while his wingman set the mess afire."

Left: Newly promoted Lt Colonel Glenn Todd Eagleston (left of the mission board) and Group CO Lt Colonel Jack Bradley (on the right) conduct an open air briefing at Ober Olm on April 17, 1945

Above The Deck—Just

"We hit the regular airfields used by the Germans so much," **recalls Richard E. Turner,** "that they were abandoning them for open fields, highways, or almost any level area close to forests which would provide camouflage. In the briefing I had made a point of discussing these hidden makeshift airdromes. It had been a while since we had been able to find any of the enemy aloft. And we determined to seek them on the ground."

On the afternoon of August 7, Richard E. Turner took off with the 356th Fighter Squadron for a sweep of the area of Chartres. "We were at 10,000ft [3,048m] when we arrived over our landmark, the famous thirteenth-century Gothic cathedral of Chartres. I turned east following a wide straight highway, inspecting its adjoining fields and forests for evidence of clandestine Luftwaffe activity. After approximately 10 miles [16km] of cruising I saw a suspicious collection of objects at the east end of a huge field bounded on two sides by woods. I approached the location for a closer look. When I descended to about 3,000ft [914m] I could see that the objects were wheat sheaves, but I could also detect the familiar outlines of an Me 109 peeking from beneath. I called my discovery to the squadron and made a firing pass on the hidden 109, getting an excellent pattern of strikes, and it exploded and burned. I pulled up and over, going for the

Above: *P-51B-5 "Peggy" in the 355th Fighter Squadron, 354th Fighter Group was one of the first Mustangs to fly in combat over occupied Europe with the "Pioneer Mustang Group" at Boxted, Essex, in December 1943.*

fringe of forest where others in the squadron had discovered more fighters parked. For the next five minutes we gave the concealed airdrome a good working over. We happily returned to our beachhead strip for landing. As we flew I tallied up the reported number of Me 109s destroyed by each pilot. The total came to at least nineteen, which made the mission a resounding success."

From the 14th through the 18th of August, Richard E. Turner flew five patrols over eastern France: "We strafed German road columns, hoping to impair the flexibility of the German High Command which was desperately trying to halt the American advance. During this period we would get heavy ground fire when occasionally bad weather conditions forced us low over the Falaise Gap area as we felt our way to the base. It was during one of these barrages that I collected a hole in my wing which was to be the second and last time I was hit by ground fire.

"On the 26th of August I took another patrol of my squadron to Reims and we surprised the airdrome at Beauvais during refueling operations. I took my whole outfit in on a pass and clobbered all the Fw 190s visible. Pulling up to the left in a circle

Left: *The Mustang's range of 2,080 miles (3,347km) was achieved by the internal fuel it carried. A total of 92 gallons (418 liters) were contained in each wing and this was supplemented by two 75-gallon (341-liter) underwing drop tanks and an 85-gallon (322-gallon) US fuselage tank (pictured on p.97).*

of the field I saw an undamaged 190 sitting in front of a hanger, so I called for one more pass over the field. Ducking down to 20ft [6m] above the deck I came in, withholding my fire until close range. When I tripped the trigger the Fw 190 exploded, creating a fire which poured into the hangar and engulfed the planes within. By now heavy ground fire had developed, threatening to pick off someone of my patrol, and I liked the odds we already had—about fifteen to nothing—and I wanted it to stay that way, so I ordered everyone to leave the area to rendezvous 10 miles [16km] west. I collected my squadron at the rendezvous point and found all Mustangs were present and accounted for. Pleased at the squadron's brilliant success I set course for our base, little realizing that I had destroyed my last German plane of the war."

Lieutenant Kenneth Harry "Ken" Dahlberg in the 354th Fighter Group claimed three kills on August 16 to earn him ace status. During a fighter sweep over the German lines in the vicinity of Dreux, France, the air controller reported that twenty Bf 109s had been sighted. As the P-51s moved to engage, another 60 enemy fighters dropped out of the overcast 3,000ft (914m) above them: "I lived a lifetime in those few minutes," said Dahlberg. "I clobbered one and he went straight into the ground burning. Everywhere you looked, there was a Mustang mixing it with three or four Jerries. I channeled up into the midst of a gaggle of 109s. I picked one and tapped him. He blew up, showering my plane with oil and debris. My visibility was almost nil due to oil on my windshield, but I managed to make out a lone 109 and headed for him. Just then I noticed my oil pressure was down. Someone must have gotten on my tail and shot at me, but in the excitement I never knew it until then. My gunsight was also out, but by watching the tracer bullets I was able to spray the 109. He blew up. Four other 109s hopped my tail at the same time and I knew I had to bail out. I headed for the clouds so that Jerry wouldn't clobber me as I got out."

Dahlberg evaded capture and rejoined his group after several days. On a later strafing mission Dahlberg reported: "I was going so fast I couldn't aim. When we reformed at 7,000ft [2,134m] we sighted 40 Fw 190s and took off after them. Two both blew up with my first burst. As I pulled up from the second one, I got on the tail of another Fw 190. As we started to climb up I cut his right wing off with my bullets. He bailed out. I looked around and saw a Fw 190 riddling a P-51, who in turn was shooting at another 190. I dropped down to give a hand, got some hits around the canopy and the Jerry went flying into the ground."

Dahlberg was shot down again, by flak, on December 26, 1944, but landed in Allied territory. He had fourteen victories when he was shot down and taken prisoner on February 14, 1945.

Gun Camera

Here we see a wing-mounted gun camera manufactured by The Morse Instrument Company of Hudson, Ohio. About once a week combat crews on bomber bases were shown films taken from the gun cameras of the American fighters, and it delighted them to see the German fighters catching hell. These also showed strafing missions and they could see that the German transport and ground installations were taking a severe beating. The gun camera footage also provided intelligence and tactical information.

The gun camera was mounted in the leading edge of the Mustang's left wing, near the wing root. This positioning enabled it to capture the most dramatic combat footage, as seen here in these stills of attacks on German airfields and installations.

A Yank In The RAF

"I was jumped by a Focke-Wulf 190 which shot my oil and glycol cooler away... My engine started to seize. I immediately straightened out, used my excess speed to gain height to about 800ft [244m] and headed for the sea off Dieppe. Just before straightening out, on my port rear quarter I saw a Fw 190 with grey smoke pouring from it heading towards a wood apparently out of control."

—Flight Lieutenant F. E. Clarke, 414 (Sarnia Imperials) Squadron RCAF, August 19, 1942

private school, he entered Yale University in September 1938, but resigned to enter the USAAC training scheme as an Aviation Cadet. He was "washed out" as a pilot but he was accepted into the RAF as a sergeant pilot in November 1942. By April 1944 he had one and two shared victories flying the Spitfire Vb and he destroyed a Bf 109 on June 17 flying the Mustang III. On July 26, 1944, 122 Squadron Mustangs were off at 18:20 hours, four of them carrying bombs, heading for the Dreux area. The weather appeared unsuitable for bombing so the formation set course for Argentan, hoping to come across enemy aircraft reported by the controller. Fifteen Fw 190s were seen southwest of Laigle, soon joined by two further groups, making a total of more than thirty. Six were claimed shot down, one probably, and six damaged. Pilot Officer Thorne claimed two destroyed and one damaged before his Mustang was damaged and he had to crash-land in a field at the southwest corner of a glider strip at St. Aubin.

His combat report gives some idea of the

Flying Officer Hollis Harry Hills was born in Baxter, Iowa on March 25, 1915, moving to California at the age of eleven. He enlisted in the RCAF in June 1940, and had the distinction of being credited with the first enemy aircraft shot down by a Mustang. Hills was flying AG470 and acting as a Weaver. On his second sortie the radio failed and he was unable to warn his flight commander when three Fw 190s attacked. He therefore engaged the enemy himself and shot one down. Hills declined to transfer to the USAAF but on November 8, 1942, transferred instead to the US Navy and he flew with carrier fighter squadrons for the remainder of the war, downing four "Zekes" and destroying three more Japanese aircraft on the ground.

James Neale "Jim" Thorne was born into a wealthy American family in Whitethorn, Rye, New York, on October 11, 1919. After attending a

Above left: Mustang I AM12 XV-X piloted by Flight Lt G. Kenning, who was one of the pilots who carried out 2 Squadron's first Mustang operation on Nov 14, 1942.

Right: This movie, made in 1941, saw Tyrone Power join the RAF after bumping into old flame Betty Grable.

trying to regain height and join the squadron 5,000ft [1,524m] above. Eventually at 7,000ft [2,133m] I lost the Huns and picked another e/a which flew across in front of me. He dived to starboard and then zoomed upwards. Following, I caught him easily on the zoom and closing to 75–100 yards [68–91m] I opened fire as he almost stalled. He attempted to half roll and in doing so I got many strikes along the length of his plane. Pieces flew off and he dived vertically. Following him down in a tight spiral he hit the ground when I was at 4000ft [1,219m]. Climbing again I looked for another e/a but there were not many left." Jim Thorne DFC was shot down and killed by flak over Velp, Holland on September 10, 1944.

Left: Mustang I AG633 XV-E on 2 Squadron RAF, airborne in July 1942.

performance advantages of the Mustang: "Picking the starboard e/a (enemy aircraft) in the smaller formation I opened fire from 55 yards [50m], 30/40 degree angle off I saw strikes on his starboard wing but then had to break as eight Huns were behind me. It became a series of breaks gradually losing height to 5,000ft [1,524m]. One e/a dived down in front of me and I got on to his tail. He broke to port and I followed. At 400 yards [364m], 50 degrees off I fired short bursts observing strikes on his tail unit. He half-rolled and dived vertically downwards; following him in

a steep diving turn I saw him dive straight into the ground. Simultaneously three Fw 190s that were above dived on me and I was hit in the starboard flap. The four of us began to mill around firing. I was

Above: A Royal Air Force Mustang I RM-G AM148 on 265 Squadron. The RAF was second only to the US Army Air Forces in the number of Mustangs used during World War II.

"Burning Out" The Gun Barrels

"There were no provisions for the pilot to select just two or four guns in the P-40, P-47, and P-51," recalled William B. Colgan. "The pilot instantly felt recoil of all guns through the airframe, most often described as 'shudder.' (In my later experiences with firing the guns of all these planes, I would rate 'shudder' as most distinctly felt in the P-51, a fraction less in the P-40 and a bit dampened, but still definitely there, in the heavier P-47.)

"Other fighters had their own sensations of gunfire. One pilot described triggering all guns and cannon in the P-39 as a 'tremendous roar and cockpit full of smoke.' 'Shudder of the guns' was common pilot lingo... 'Walking' fire across the ground and through targets encouraged pilots to hold the trigger down in long bursts. This often 'burned out' gun barrels. Once that was done, effective fire was lost for that mission.

"Barrels had to be replaced on the ground... six-gun P-40s and P-51s put 80 bullets per second into a target; the eight-gun P-47 put 106 per second. I put one short burst (one to two seconds) at boresight range into a German half-track. There was a bright flash as bullets hit the thing. It actually bounced and moved; pieces and parts flew off and a gaping hole nearly cut it in two. However, many pilots did not experience these things until on a combat mission. They arrived at their overseas unit with only stateside ground gunnery training..."

On September 12, 1944, the 354th Fighter Group carried out a sweep over Koblenz and nearby Linburg airfield, where two flights from the 353rd Fighter Squadron strafed Ju 88s and Fw 190s parked on the edge of the field, destroying eight of them. 2nd Lieutenant Bruce Carr had set fire to two Ju 88s during the strafing run on the airfield and had followed his flight up to 9,000ft (2,743m) when the Fw 190s were sighted. He later reported: "My flight was closest to them so I made a bounce on the rear of the enemy formation. At this point Lieutenant John E. Miller left my flight and was not seen after that. The Fw 190 that I picked out broke in a sharp climbing turn to the left. I fired a 30° deflection shot from 150 to 100 yards [137–91m]. I got many strikes on the left wing and around the engine. This ship seemed to explode and became enveloped in flames. The pilot immediately bailed out. I then saw a lone Fw 190 on the deck trying to get away from the fight. I dived after him and fired a short burst at about 30° deflection from about 250 yards [229m]. I saw a few strikes and he started a turn to the left. I closed to about 150 yards [137m], fired again and got strikes on his engine and around the cockpit. As I fired he snapped to the left on his back and flew into a hill."

On October 29, 1944, Major Glenn Todd Eagleston led the 354th Fighter Group on a dive-bombing and fighter sweep. The Mustangs were on course at 11:30 hours when a large gaggle of bogeys was called in at 9 o'clock. Eagleston reported: "I waited until the enemy gaggle had almost set itself for a bounce and called a group turn of 180° to the left in order to meet the e/a [enemy aircraft] head-on. I ordered the group to

Left: The six .50-caliber machines guns used in the P-51D. The cartridge belts represent the amount of ammunition used by one gun on a flight. Thirty-six men would be needed to carry the amount of ammunition as this is only one-sixth of the total used by all six guns

This pilot was particularly aggressive and showed no desire to run. I was also amazed at the performance of his aircraft, which showed climbing and turning ability far above any Me 109 that I had ever encountered. I rat-raced like that with him about five minutes without getting into shooting position. Finally, he pulled straight up and I closed to about 100 yards [91m] and fired a two-second burst, scoring many strikes on the fuselage. He started to smoke badly and a few pieces came off. He fell into a spin and burst into flame. I observed this e/a crash and explode.

"By this time the enemy were split up and coming from all directions so that it was very necessary to keep looking around. My wingman, Lieutenant Frederick I. Couch, had been unable to release his bombs and in spite of this fact he had stayed in excellent cover position through severe

Left: Armorers feed belts of .50-caliber ammunition into the Mustang's machine guns in the left wing. Toward the end of 1943, criticisms of the P-51B's firepower induced North American to increase armament from four to six wing guns and improve ammunition stowage.

Below: Browning M2 .50-caliber machine guns from the crashed aircraft "Little Zippie," with ammo belt.

jettison bombs armed and proceeded to attack. The e/a formation was very well spread out and semi-line abreast in flights of four and eight; estimated number, 60-plus. I encountered a single 109 at about 10,000ft [3,048m] and tacked on, but had trouble catching him so I fired a short burst at 45° without observing strikes. I then fired a one-second burst at 30° and observed strikes on fuselage and left wing root and the e/a started smoking. After this I pulled astern, zero degrees, and fired a two second burst from about 200 yards [183m]. The e/a started to burn and the pilot bailed. Observing a flight of four Me 109s at 11,000ft [3,353m], I bounced them and fired a one-second burst at the No. 4 man, observing a few strikes on his fuselage. The e/a broke into me and started a climbing turn.

and violent maneuvering, making it possible for me to concentrate on my targets. I observed a single Me 109 at about 10,000ft [3,048m], slightly above and climbing, going in the opposite direction. I pulled up underneath him with the e/a almost in a loop and fired a two-second burst from about 100 yards [91m] at about 90° deflection, scoring many strikes directly beneath the cockpit. He started to burn and fell off into a spin. The pilot bailed and the aircraft crashed and exploded."

Eagleston's most successful mission against the Luftwaffe moved his score up to 16.5 enemy aircraft destroyed in the air. The 354th was forced to give up its beloved Mustangs in mid-December 1944 and did not get them back until mid-February 1945.

Tuskegee Airmen

"Fueled by bias from above, they [white bomber unit crews] expressed outrage that a few ignorant do-gooders would put the lives of white American soldiers in jeopardy by assigning the 332nd Fighter Group to escort them. Having come this far, the Tuskegee Airmen faced two enemies and one was American."

—From *Tuskegee Airman* by Charlene E. McGee Smith Ph.D.

In 1939 blacks were admitted into the Civil Pilot Training Program at six black colleges and two non-academic flying schools. On January 16, 1941, against the wishes of the War Department Congress, the 99th Fighter Squadron was created. The first all-black fighter squadron was activated at Tuskegee Army Air Field in Macon County, Alabama, near the town of Tuskegee and the Tuskegee Institute.

Basic training began with just thirteen cadets. Lieutenant Colonel Benjamin O. Davis Jr., a professional soldier with a West Point education, led the 99th Fighter Squadron, and on April 14, 1943, the squadron left Tuskegee for the 12th Air Force in the Mediterranean Theater of Operations. By May 1943, the orientation phase ended and the 99th flew its first combat mission against enemy positions on the island of Pantelleria in the Mediterranean Sea on June 6. By the fall of 1943, the 99th Fighter Squadron had moved to Licata, Sicily, and the pilots flew many patrol and strike missions against Axis supply lines and communications centers. By September the 99th had moved to Paestum airfield near Salerno.

Lieutenant Colonel Davis now assumed command of the 332nd Fighter Group, comprising the 99th, 100th, 301st, and 302nd Fighter Squadrons. The group's pilots

Left: *Lieutenant Wendell Pruit and his crew chief in front of the red-tailed 332nd Fighter Group P-51D "Alice – Jo." A crew chief maintained "his" Mustang with pride and diligence.*

were well-trained, with experience flying the P-47 Thunderbolt, P-40, and P-39 Airacobra fighters. In January 1944, the Tuskegee Airmen downed eight enemy aircraft over the beachhead at Anzio in one day. In a two-week period, the 99th achieved a seven-to-one kill ratio in air combat and Army Air Forces commander Henry "Hap" Arnold awarded the 99th an official commendation.

By April the squadron was attached to the 324th Fighter Group and it took part in Operation *Strangle*, the air campaign to isolate the besieged German defenders in the battle for Monte Cassino. On June 6, the 332nd was attached to the 15th Air Force and began the transition to P-51C-10s, which were soon painted with the distinctive red tail livery. On June 7, 1944, the Tuskegee Airmen moved to Ramitelli in central Italy, near the Adriatic, where they would remain until VE Day. Although segregated and isolated, Ramatelli, with its runway constructed with perforated steel matting, was ideal for the black airmen to rendezvous quickly with bombers of the 15th Air Force en route to targets in Germany and Central Europe. In July Davis led the first bomber escort mission. Davis insisted that his fighter escorts never leave the bombers, stay close in and provide proper defense. He did not allow his pilots to abandon escort duty for any targets of opportunity. One result of this practice was the high regard B-24 crews had for the black airmen, who routinely offered close support on all missions deep into enemy territory.

Victories

With the freedom to pursue and destroy enemy fighters, the 332nd's victories mounted quickly. On June 9, 1944, the Red Tails scored five victories in one day. Lieutenant (later Captain) Wendell Pruitt of St. Louis, Missouri, in the 302nd Fighter Squadron was credited with the first kill. He described what happened: "We were assigned to fly top cover for heavy bombers. On approaching the Udine area, a flock of Me 109s was observed making attacks from 5 o'clock on a formation of B-24s. Each enemy aircraft made a pass at the bombers and fell into a left rolling turn. I rolled over, shoved everything forward and closed in on a 109 at about 475mph [764kmph]. I waited as he shallowed out of a turn, gave him a couple of two-second bursts, and watched him explode."

The Tuskegee pilots found that the P-51 was much more maneuverable than their earlier P-47s. They easily climbed to over 30,000ft (9,144m), which allowed the fighters to rise with the bombers above the range of flak. "We would get into a scrap ... zooming around up there in the air pretty close to each other at some pretty good speeds," recalled 2nd Lieutenant Charles E. McGee. When Charles flew his first mission escorting bombers to Munich, he felt like they were finally doing the job they had come to do. On July 4 he flew his first long-range mission in P-51C 42-103072 *Kitten*, escorting bombers to Romania. "They knew when they had Red Tails flying with them, they had protection from the Germans they could count on. Colonel Davis instilled in us that our mission was to protect those bombers from enemy fighters... if we heard German aircraft in the air and they weren't attacking the bomb group, we didn't go off looking for them. We stayed with the bombers. Everyone was swivel neck ... constantly looking."

P-51s had two drop tanks holding 65 gallons (246 liters) of fuel each, enough to support missions of four-and-a-half to six-and-a-half hours, depending on weather, altitude, targets, and resistance encountered. Bombers were slower and their missions at times exceeded ten hours. "Ten minutes would go by and you'd still be looking at the same mountain. You had no idea what in the world was going on," commented Charles. All the missions were long flights, usually five hours and more. On those flights, Charles found the cockpit small. "You can sweat through a leather flight jacket sitting up there in the sun." **On long flights like that, he was glad to get off target and relax a bit in less rigid formation on the way**

Keep us flying!

BUY WAR BONDS

Left: "Keep us Flying": a Tuskegee Buy War Bonds poster. War bonds were a debt security (essentially a loan to the government) issued by the US administration to raise finance for military equipment and operations. The bonds matured in ten years, at which point the purchaser received the original sum plus interest.

Right: A P-51 "Red Tail" signed by surviving Tuskegee Airmen, located at the Palm Springs Air Museum.

back. In September 1944, Charles was promoted to 1st lieutenant, becoming a flight leader in the 302nd Fighter Squadron.

On July 12, 1944, Captain Joseph D. Elsberry from Langston, Oklahoma became the first black pilot to score three kills in one day. Eight days later Elsberry scored his fourth victory while escorting B-24s of the 47th Bomb Wing in the Munich area. While in pursuit of still another enemy aircraft, he was forced to pull up to avoid running into a mountain peak.

"This was the last time I engaged an enemy aircraft at close range," said Elsberry, "and my failure to register this victory meant the difference of being cited as an ace."

On July 17, the Tuskegee Airmen escorted the 306th Bomb Wing on a bombing mission to the Avignon railroad marshaling yard and railroad bridge in southern France. Nineteen Bf 109s appeared but only three attacked the Liberators in the 459th Bomb Group and they split-S'ed away at the sight of the P-51s descending on them, and then made a series of evasive left turns. Luther "Quibbling" Smith, Robert "Dissiparin" Smith, and Larry Wilkins closed in and shot down the 109s, following them all the way down. 2nd Lieutenant Maceo Harris recalled: "My flight leader and I went down on two bogeys, and after they split-S'ed from me at about 18,000ft [5,486m], I pulled up all alone in a tight chandelle to the left. I tried to join another ship, but lost him when I peeled

Left: Lieutenant Edward C. Gleed briefs pilots in the 332nd Fighter Group in Italy in September 1944.

Below: *Pfc John Fields in the 332nd Fighter Group loads the wing guns of a P-51B. Behind him is the P-51D "Stinky." The 57-inch (145cm) long Browning gun first appeared in 1921 and it was produced in greater numbers han any other US machine gun in WWII. It fired at a rate of 550 rounds per minute.*

off on two more bogeys that were after some bombers. The bogeys turned steeply to the left, and P-51s were in the vicinity, so I kept on with the bombers because they were hitting the target. Flak was intense over the target and I kept an eye on the B-24s for enemy fighters that might come in when the bombers left the area.

"Upon leaving the target, I joined another P-51 and tried to contact him by radio. My attempt was unsuccessful, so I peeled off alone on three bogeys who were approaching a straggling bomber from the rear. They looked like P-51s and I rocked my wings coming in, but they swung left over France away from the bomber. I widely circled the B-24 because the top turret gunner was firing at me, but when he stopped firing I came in very close to survey the flak damage. The number two engine was feathered and the number one was smoking moderately."

The B-24 made a two-wheel recovery and Harris landed as well. "The B-24 pilot was Lieutenant Loerb from San Francisco," said Harris. "The ship was 41-29585. He and the co-pilot appreciated my friendly aid and kissed me after the manner of the French."

During that summer and fall of 1944 the Tuskegee Airmen flew a series of diverse missions against the Axis air forces. In July there was a high-risk mission to the German-controlled Ploesti oil refineries in Romania, which were a fiercely defended fuel source for the entire German military. In August, the 332nd flew repeated sorties as escorts for bombing raids to support the invasion of southern France. There was even an escort mission to Czechoslovakia. Luke Weathers and two other Tuskegee Airmen escorted a crippled B-24 bomber to safety in England. Weathers downed two Bf 109s.

Pursuit

On July 18, 1944, Lieutenant Clarence D. "Lucky" Lester was flying his P-51 Mustang *Miss Pelt* when he notched three victories in one day. "It was a clear day. Our mission was to rendezvous over northern Italy's Po Valley at 25,000ft [7,620m] with B-17s en route to bomb a German airfield in southern Germany. We had been given the task of escorting the bombers to the target and back, providing protection from enemy aircraft. We relished the assignment since it allowed us to conduct a fighter sweep, which meant we provided general cover, but had no specific group of 'Forts' to protect.

"I flew with the 100th Fighter Squadron. The name 'Lucky' stuck because of all the tight situations from which I had escaped without a scratch or even a bullet hole in my aircraft.

"The rendezvous was made on time at 25,000ft [7,620m]. The bombers always came in higher than planned and continued to climb so that they reached the target well over 30,000ft [9,144m] (the higher, the safer from ground fire). The other squadrons of the 332nd began their close cover at 27,000ft [8,230m]. We were around 29,000ft [8,839m] when bogeys [enemy aircraft] were spotted above us.

"We were flying a loose combat formation, 200ft [61m] apart and zig-zagging. The flight leader commanded 'hard right turn and punch tanks' [drop external fuel tanks] when Number Four called that he could not get one of his two tanks off. He was never seen again. At this time, I saw a formation of Messerschmitt Bf 109s straight ahead, but slightly lower. I closed to about 200ft [61m] and started to fire. Smoke began to pour out of the 109 and the aircraft exploded. I was going so fast I was sure I would hit some of the debris from the explosion, but luckily I didn't.

"As I was dodging pieces of aircraft, I saw another 109 to my right, all alone on a heading 90° to mine, but at the same altitude. I turned onto his tail and closed to about 200ft [61m] while firing. His aircraft started to smoke and almost stopped. My closure was so fast I began to overtake him. When I overran him, I looked down to see the enemy pilot emerge

Right: Lieutenant Colonel Benjamin Davis, commanding the 99th Fighter Squadron, seen here in the cockpit of his P-51. Davis had a distinguished wartime service, and later he rose to become the first African-American general in the US Air Force.

Left: On March 29, 2007, about 350 Tuskegee airmen (or their widows) received the Congressional Gold Medal for their bravery in World War II. The original is at the Smithsonian. This one is one of the bronze replicas given to individual recipients.

from his burning aircraft. I remember seeing his blonde hair as he bailed out at approximately 8,000ft [2,438m].

"By this time, I was alone and looking for my flight mates when I spotted the third 109 flying very low, about 1,000ft [914m] off the ground. I dove to the right behind him and opened fire. As I scored hits, he apparently thought he had enough altitude to use a split-S maneuver to evade me. [A 'split-S' is a one-half loop going down; the aircraft is rolled upside down and pulled straight through until it is right side up—not recommended below 3,500ft/1,067m.]

"We were approximately 1,000ft [305m] above the ground and, as I did a diving turn, I saw the 109 go straight into the ground. During the return flight, it took a while to realize how much had happened in that brief span

Above: *A group of the 322nd Fighter Group pilots in Italy in August 1944 "shoot the breeze" in the shadow of one of their P-51 Mustangs.*

Right: *Reverse of the Congressional Gold Medal for the Tuskegee bravery in World War II. This one is one of the bronze replicas given to individual recipients.*

formation and he pursued. Before Charles knew it he was in the middle of a dogfight. From training and instinct, Charles put his P-51 through dives, banks and climbs, taking evasive action while maneuvering for position.

"We were over the local airfield. As we flashed over the field proper in a right turn, out of the corner of my eye I saw that there was a hangar and several aircraft fires brightly burning." Executing a roll, Charles was able to get on his enemy's tail. With his wingman 2nd Lieutenant Roger Romine flying cover to protect his flank, Charles fired a burst that found its mark. The disabled plane lost control and began to drop from the sky, careened across the airfield, and exploded in flames at its perimeter. "Must have hit something in the controls. He took a couple hard evasive turns and went right into the ground." After downing the Fw 190 Charles stayed low. "I made a low-altitude dash out of the area to avoid ground fire and for good measure dropped my nose to make a firing pass and make a good burst on a locomotive at a railroad stop before climbing to rejoin the group."

of time [4–6 minutes maximum]. Everything went the same as in training except for the real bullets. Real Bullets!!! Until then the danger of this mission had never occurred to me."

In the aftermath, Charles performed the textbook check of his aircraft to see if everything was okay. Those brief moments and his instinctive response were what all the training and preparation had been about. In the most challenging aerial combat, he had measured up. He was the one going home. The kill was Charles's first aerial victory.

In October 1944, Lester shot down three German fighters in one day. He was awarded the Distinguished Flying Cross and went on to fly in the post-war US Air Force.

Charles McGee recalled the August 24 mission when fifty-two P-51s escorted bombers of the 5th Bomb Wing to a Czechoslovakian oil refinery and Pardubice airdrome north of Vienna. As the bombers approached, several German aircraft managed to get off the ground and, once airborne, mounted an attack. Charles McGee got the word to respond and turned his flight into the attack. One Fw 190 broke

The 302nd's 1st Lieutenant William H. Thomas got another Fw 190 and 1st Lieutenant John F. Briggs of the 100th Squadron downed a Bf 109 on that mission. Regrettably, Roger Romine was later killed in an on-the-ground plane collision following his 97th mission on November 16, 1944. On September 8, in a fighter sweep over an enemy airfield at Ilandza, Yugoslavia, Charles McGee damaged a number of enemy aircraft on the ground and was credited with destroying one. Missions eventually brought a ticket home for Charles and others.

Flying Faster Than My Bullets

On August 12 1944, seventy-one P-51s in the 332nd split into a trio of attacking sections for pre-selected strafing missions against enemy radar stations in southern France. Sweeping in, the P-51s attacked at levels ranging from 2,000 to 500ft (610 to 152m), to just a few feet from the ground. There was no interference from enemy aircraft, but the ground fire and flak was extremely heavy and deadly. Woodrow W. Crockett of the 100th Squadron, 332nd Fighter Group, remembered one operation: "We liked to hit targets going out to sea, but on this mission we had to go inland. After the mission, I called for a 90° turn to the right. We were on deck. I called for the second 90° turn which would take us out to sea. Halfway through my turn to get us out of France, I saw a lookout tower in Marseilles Harbor. It looked like that tower on a can of cleanser. I rolled out and said, 'Look what I found.' I sprayed it from bottom to top and then I decided I better break. The controls were awfully stiff.

"When I did break, it sounded like I went through a tunnel. I thought that I had lost the scoop of my Mustang, that's how close I was. The instruments were still reading. If I hit the tower, I'd planned on going right on over and crash-landing on land. I went on out to sea and I could see them shooting at me with holes back here in the seven o'clock position. I looked at my airspeed and I was still doing 425mph [684kmph] and I said, 'If I can do this for another minute, I'll be seven miles out to sea, out of range'. We came back; we lost six people on that mission. Jefferson from Detroit was one of those guys. We came back to base. Major Mattison got his tail almost shot off; all his cables were exposed. A couple of times they had us as MIAs [Missing in Action], but we made it back."

Hiram Mann, a 302nd Fighter Squadron pilot, explains the shock of return fire: "Most of our missions were due north and we would rendezvous with the bombers and head on to wherever our target was. We were escort and would always fly above the bombers. When the bombers started their bomb run, we would leave them and fly a wide pattern around their target area, and when they rallied off the target area, we would pick them up again. We were seldom in any position to be shot at.

"On my first strafing mission, I put two ticks of gum in my mouth before I got in my plane and hooked up my oxygen mask. We took off and were flying over and the flight leader called for us to jettison our external tanks

Left: Here, S/Sgt Bill Accoo, 99th Fighter Squardon, washes the waxed surface of the P-51C with soap and water. Waxing helped smooth the air flow and added more speed. When camouflage paint was deleted from factory production it was estimated that the reduced drag and weight added an extra 5mph (8kmph) to top speed. Above: Three Tuskegee ground crew jockey an auxiliary fuel tank into position beneath the wing of the Mustang.

Left: *Angle-head flashlight adopted in 1941. Various models along with numerous variations were used during WWII. The TL122A model here was painted olive drab and was used in Africa and the Mediterranean.*

Right: *Lieutenant Colonel Lee Archer died January 27, 2010, aged ninety. He was a member of the famed Tuskegee Airmen and flew some 169 combat missions during World War II.*

and he picked out a target. He saw a train rolling on the ground. We got into echelon and went in. The leader went for the engine. As you spread out, you pick out a boxcar and you start firing on the car. I picked out my car and gave my plane full throttle. I'm in my dive and I aimed on this boxcar and I squeezed my trigger.

"We had three .50-caliber guns in each wing and they converged at 250 yards [229m] in front. Every fifth bullet in the gun is a tracer. It lights up as it goes out. I could see my tracers as they were going. The adrenaline is pumping. And then I saw tracer marks going past me. The first thought was 'I'm flying faster than my bullets.' Then it occurred to me, 'They're shooting at me!' This was not the scenario that you got in ground school. My plane was struck, but I was not shot down. When we got back I got out on the wing. You don't get nervous until after the excitement is over. I had literally chewed that gum to the point that there was no cohesion. I had a mouth full of little BBs."

Lieutenant (later Captain) Louis Purnell described what it felt like to kill an enemy pilot on a strafing mission. "After returning to the base I checked the aircraft—a brand new P-51 on its maiden combat mission—for bullet holes. Hanging over the edge of the airscoop beneath the place was a strange object—a black-brownish glob, wet in some spots. I poked at it with a stick, and it fell to the ground... Then it dawned on me: this was part of a man... My first thought was better he than me, but then I started thinking seriously about what had happened. Eighty minutes ago that man was alive and healthy and whole. His parents had raised him just as mine had raised me. He had nothing against me and I had nothing against him, but since our countries were at war, killing was legal. When called to arms, one must defend his country ... but it all seemed so futile."

1st Lieutenant Jack D. Holsclaw, the Assistant Group Operations Officer, reported on the mission on September 2: "Four squadrons covered strafing area, highway and RR [railroad] installations along highway from Stalak to Cuprija and north toward Belgrade. No troops, truck convoys or railway movements were seen. The other two squadrons turned left and followed the highway from Stalak to Krusevac to Kraljivo to Kragujevac. Sighting nothing they took a course east to Cuprija and followed the highway north from that point. No enemy traffic was sighted. One pilot taking off late attempted to catch the formation. He never did catch up and saw a convoy of 30 trucks. He strafed them, setting three on fire and damaged ten more. On his route home he saw no traffic of any kind, troops, trucks, or trains."

Apache

"The A-24 was a good, stable airplane. But it was too slow for the kind of flying we were expecting in Italy against the Luftwaffe's Me 109s and Fw 190s. I think the decision to go to the A-36 was because that airplane could act in both capacities, it really was the ideal fighter-bomber."

—Roland W. Tapp, 27th Fighter Group (Dive)

RAF adoption of the Mustang for use in a ground-attack role had brought USAAF procurement in spring 1942 of 500 of the A-36A version for dive-bombing, fitted with wing-mounted air-brakes. It was named Apache initially, but later adopted the British name Mustang. "Dutch" Kindelberger convinced General Arnold that the P-51A's single .50- and two .30-caliber wing guns on the RAF Mustangs should be replaced by six .50-caliber Browning machine guns; two in each wing and two mounted in the engine fairing, firing through the propeller arc. These guns had to be cocked in the cockpit, but were fired from the same trigger as the others. North American made only 500 A-36s. Three groups formerly using the

Vengeance two-seaters went into combat with the A-36A. They were the first USAAF Mustangs to see combat, equipping two groups in Sicily and Italy in 1943. The first P-51A group was the 54th, which remained in Florida for replacement training, while later P-51As went to the China–Burma–India (CBI) theater in India for the 23rd, 311th, and 1st Air Commando Groups and flew their first missions on Thanksgiving Day 1943. When these aircraft were all shot down, crashed or otherwise used up, the combat units went first to old P-40s, then to either P-47s or P-51s. There were no more A-36s and no more true dive-bombers in the USAAF. All genuine dive-bomber pilots did not consider a 45–60° dive to be a real dive!

Combat missions against Sicily, Pantelleria, and Lampedusa were begun from Tunisia on June 6, 1943, by the 27th Fighter Group (re-designated the 27th Fighter-Bomber Group in August), joined by the A-36As of the 86th Bombardment Group (Dive) (soon named 86th Fighter-Bomber Group/FBG) in July. Both groups were among the aircraft that supported *Husky* landings on Sicily before taking part in the Italian campaign that followed. Despite some heavy losses, the A-36As wrought tremendous

Left: *A-36As being serviced at a base in the southeast United States.*

Inset above: *A-36A Apaches being bombed up ready for a mission. The A-36 flew their first combat sorties over Pantellaria, Italy on June 6, 1943.*

havoc. Every conceivable type of target was attacked, from troops and vehicles of the Hermann Göring Division to flak batteries and railroad marshaling yards. An American war correspondent, reporting on the A-36A, cabled "The scream of this plane when it dives would shake any man. It makes a Stuka sound like an alley cat. When it levels off at the bottom and lands those bombs right on target, it zooms away as a heavily-gunned fighter, looking for Axis troops to strafe, for enemy planes or tanks or trains to destroy. It's a hot ship ... plenty fast and plenty rugged. No wonder our jubilant pilots nicknamed it 'Invader.'"

On September 10, 1943, the 27th FBG prevented three German Panzer divisions from reaching the Salerno beach-head; this earned the group a Distinguished Unit Citation. Another outstanding feat by the A-36A was the sinking by two aircraft that same month of a 50,000-ton Italian transport vessel of the Conti Di Savoia class while it was riding at anchor at Baguara. The A-36As flew 23,373 sorties and dropped more than 16,000 bombs before being replaced by P-47s in 1944.

In India the A-36A was operated by the 311th FBG. They were the only liquid-cooled attack aircraft and the last dive-bombers used in the war by the Army Air Force. Their success demonstrated the value of single-seat fighter-bombers and led to widespread use of later P-51 and P-47 models on close-support missions.

Right: NAA poster extolling the capabilities of the A-36, which for a short time was dubbed "the Invader" by its pilots in the 12th Air Force.

Below: The RAF received one solitary A-36A (EW998) fitted with dive brakes in the upper wing trailing edges, to flight test and evaluate.

Yank pilots nicknamed it "Invader"

During the fierce battles for Sicily and Italy, a brilliantly engineered new plane speeded our victory.

Officially known as the A-36, the new North American fighter-bomber was adapted from the famous P-51 Mustang. An American correspondent, reporting on this sensational new ship, cabled:

"The scream of this plane when it dives would shake any man. It makes a Stuka sound like an alley cat.

"When it levels off at the bottom, and lays those bombs right on the target, it zooms away as a heavily-gunned fighter, looking for Axis troops to strafe, for enemy planes or tanks or trains to destroy. It's a hot ship ... plenty fast and plenty rugged. No wonder our jubilant pilots nicknamed it 'Invader.'"

But perhaps more important than its destructive power is the way the Mustang saves lives ... the lives of *our* soldiers. Blast the enemy's planes out of the air ... disrupt his communications ..., devastate his supply depots and transportation ... destroy his offensive power ... and you make the task of our ground forces infinitely easier, safer. With air superiority, it's as simple as that.

Through constantly improved designs, and field service on every fighting front, the men and women of North American Aviation are enabled to set the pace in an industry which safeguards America's future. The more and better planes they build, the sooner Axis resistance will be smashed ... and the more American lives will be spared.

North American Aviation, Inc., designers and builders of the B-25 Mitchell bomber, AT-6 Texan trainer and the P-51 Mustang fighter (A-36 fighter-bomber). Member of Aircraft War Production Council, Inc.

North American Aviation *Sets the Pace!*

Red Tails In The Sunset

In October 1944, the 332nd lost fifteen pilots in air combat. In a notable October mission, seventy-two aircraft from the 332nd flew north for strafing attacks along the River Danube from Budapest, Hungary, to Bratislava, Czechoslovakia. With heavy cloud cover, only thirty aircraft managed to reach the target area where they strafed three enemy airfields along the Danube. The next day Wendell Pruitt set off to down a He 111, only to be attacked suddenly by seven Bf 109s from his lower-left side. Lee "Buddy" Archer, who had already scored two victories for the Tuskegee Airmen, was flying wingman for Wendell Pruitt. Lieutenant Archer described the dogfight: "We had just crossed Lake Balaton, when I spied a group of enemy aircraft at two o'clock high and climbing. Two Messerschmitts were flying abreast. I tore the wing off one with a long burst. The other slid in behind Pruitt. I pulled up, zeroed in, hit the gun button and watched him explode."

Pruitt was chasing an enemy aircraft when his guns jammed. Archer followed the enemy aircraft as it took a sharp dive. "I don't know whether he was damaged by Pruitt or not," said Archer, "but he appeared to be trying to land. I opened up at ground level, hit him with a long volley and he crashed. Flak and small arms fire forced me out of there in a hurry." Pruitt downed one He 111 and one fighter. Archer downed three Bf 109s. Six other Tuskegee pilots scored a single air victory, with only one loss the 332nd returned home with a total of nine kills for the day. Six of the nine Bf 109s and all three Heinkel He 111s had been shot down in just fifteen minutes.

Above, inset: Lieutenant Andrew D. Marshal in the 322nd Fighter Group with bandaged head, an injury suffered after after flak downed his Mustang during a strafing run. Local Greeks hid him from the Germans

Right: Captain Andrew D. Turner. Turner was commander of the 100th Fighter Squadron, 332nd Fighter Group, 15th Air Force. He graduated from Tuskegee class 42-I-SE and was inducted on October 9, 1942.

In his year-end message to his men, Group Commander Colonel Davis said: "I cannot fail to mention the all-important fact that your achievements have been recognized. Unofficially you are known by an untold number of bomber crews as those who can be depended upon and whose appearance means certain protection from enemy fighters. The bomber crews have told others of your accomplishments, and your good reputation has preceded you in many parts where you may think you are unknown. The Commanding General of the Fifteenth Fighter Command has stated that we are doing a good job and thus, the official report of our operations is a creditable one."

Flying fighter escort for the 15th Air Force became the prime task for the 332nd in 1945. In January bad weather limited the 332nd to just eleven missions. In February thirty-nine missions were flown. On March 24, Davis led Red Tail escorts to support a 15th Air Force mission to attack the Daimler-Benz factory in Berlin, a 1,600-mile (2,575km) round trip. Colonel Davis's Mustang Bennie developed engine trouble which forced him

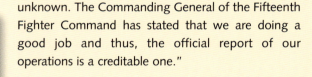

to return to base, leaving Captain Armor McDaniel in command. Over Berlin the airmen of the 332nd encountered twenty-five German attackers, many flying Me 262 jet aircraft. Seeing one for the first time a pilot said: "It flew past us so fast, we never got a chance to call it in."

The jets were flown by largely inexperienced pilots and three of the German jets were shot down by Roscoe C. Brown, Charles Brantly and Earl Lane; three black pilots also died. (Prior to this Allied pilots had downed only two jets). As a consequence of this mission the 332nd received a Distinguished Unit Citation.

On March 31 the Red Tails went on a strafing mission near Linz, Austria, where they met seventeen Me 262s and Focke-Wulf 190s. The Tuskegee Airmen shot down thirteen of the jets without loss. On April 1, the Tuskegee Airmen provided escort for the 47th Bomber Wing in a mission to bomb the railroad marshaling yards in Polten, Austria. When they were returning home, the black pilots spotted four enemy Fw 190s below the bomber formation. They dove on the enemy aircraft only to realize that they had been drawn into a trap. Suddenly other Luftwaffe aircraft appeared and in the melée that followed no fewer than twelve enemy fighters were shot down, while three Red Tail Mustangs were lost. Later in April the 332nd destroyed the last four enemy aircraft in the Mediterranean Theater to take their impressive tally to 111 enemy aircraft downed in air combat and another 150 destroyed on the ground. The 332nd had lost a total of sixty-six pilots for all causes, in the States and in the theaters of war. Thirty-two black airmen had been shot down and captured.

One PoW who was interviewed after the war said: "I expected to be treated badly. Instead I was treated like an officer... I was amazed at how much the German Stalag commanders knew about us [the Red Tails]. They opened a file that was full of information about our group." **The black PoWs were asked repeatedly why they would risk their lives for a country that did not respect them as men. Another Tuskegee Airman, who survived part of World War II in a German prison camp, attended a college presentation at Ohio University, a young student in the audience asked if the pilot had ever been afraid during his assignments.** "If I ever felt fear, I would have climbed out of the cockpit without hesitation and returned to quarters," was the airman's reply. "Up there you're no good to yourself or anyone else if you have doubts and you had better understand that. As hard as things were, there (in the camp) I was not black or white. Just another American pilot and officer afforded the same treatment as the others. That was better than I got when I was freed and returned to my own country after the war."

The Heraldry of the Sky

The Tuskegee Airmen's shield is azure on a fess nebule or, a panther passant sable armed and incensed gules with the motto "SPIT FIRE," which was officially approved on January 15, 1943.

The squadrons that made up the group were the 99th (below—a golden-orange winged panther); the 100th (bottom—a crouching tan and brown panther); the 301st (a caricatured cat wearing a red cape, brown aviator's helmet and white goggles piloting a gray .50-caliber machine gun with red and white tail); and the 302nd (a Red Devil with a white and yellow pitchfork with skull on the tip of the handle).

Left: The golden-orange winged panther of the 99th Fighter Squadron, 332nd Fighter Group.

Right: The crouching tan and brown panther of the 100th Fighter Squadron, 332nd Fighter Group.

Battles with the Luftwaffe

"On our return flight we were chased by two Mustangs. They came closer but did not fire; they had probably exhausted their ammunition. One of them flew in a curve to dead ahead of my Me 410; the pilot waved and I instinctively pressed my firing button. He burst apart. I could weep even today when I think about it."

—Unteroffizier Walter Ibold, Bf 110 and Me 410 *Zerstörer* pilot, ZG 76, in the *Reichsverteidigung* (Defense of the Reich), 1944

Despite the Allies' best efforts, German production of fighter aircraft actually increased through 1944 into 1945. It had peaked in September 1944, when 1,874 Bf 109s and 1,002 Fw 190s were completed, though in that same month an average of three German fighters—and two pilots—were lost for every B-17 or B-24 shot down. Even so, the Allied heavy bombing raids and strafing missions by the US and RAF fighter forces had virtually grounded the Luftwaffe fighter arm and the only units able to operate until final defeat were the jet- and rocket-powered fighters.

On November 2 the defending 8th Air Force Mustangs routed their German attackers and the 352nd Fighter Group established a record thirty-eight kills on that occasion. When Mustang pilots and their German adversaries in Bf 109s and Fw 190s were pitched against each other experience—or the lack of it—was often the deciding factor. By 1943–44 American Mustang pilots confronted scores of German *Experten* that had been in continuous action in Europe since 1940. Apart from a few pilots who flew in the RAF "Eagle" squadrons equipped with Spitfires, USAAF pilots from 1942 onwards were relatively new to their trade and were not combat-capable. Skill in aerial combat meant flying a fighter

Left: The P-51D "Big Beautiful Doll" at Duxford; it was flown by Colonel John Landers, who was the CO of 78th Fighter Group from February 22 to July 1, 1945.

aircraft to its limit not only of performance but of handling, and when the performance of the enemy was equal to that of the P-51 pilot then handling characteristics became vital in seeking an advantage.

Between January and April 1944, the Luftwaffe day-fighter arm lost over 1,000 pilots, which included the core of experienced fighter leaders. III./JG 3, for instance, was decimated during 8–17 July. For four victory claims, the *Gruppe* lost ten pilots killed or missing in action, plus two PoWs, and 18 Bf 109s were destroyed.

The USSTAF was clearly winning the battle of attrition in the war against the Luftwaffe. January 1945 marked the 8th Air Force's third year of operations and it seemed as if the end of the war was in sight. The Wehrmacht advance in the Ardennes came to a halt and ultimately petered out. The Luftwaffe, however, was still far from defeated. In the east the Red Army prepared for the great winter offensive, which would see the capture of Warsaw and Krakow and take the Soviets across the German border. Germany had no reserves left. Hitler's last chance now lay in his so-called "wonder weapons": the V-1 pilotless flying bomb and the V-2 sub-orbital rocket. V-1s killed more than 6,000 civilians and nearly 18,000 were injured. The flying bombs traveled at 400mph (644kmph) and nearly 2,500 of these weapons fell on London and the same amount on unfortunate Antwerp, Belgium, after its capture by Allied ground troops.

Writing On The Wall For The Luftwaffe

Oberleutnant Otto "Stotto" Stammberger, Staffelkapitän, 2./JGr West, knew that the writing was on the wall for the German day fighter arm. "I knew from the reports of my comrades, that after the American long-range fighters, the Thunderbolt, Mustang, and also the Lightning, entered the fray, it was no longer possible to get at the bomber *'Pulks'* [formations] without suffering grievous losses."

Leutnant Walther Hagenah, IV. Sturm/JG 3, served as a pilot in the Luftwaffe day-fighter arm from spring 1942 and flew operationally almost without a break until the end of the war. He was shot down three times. "On 12 May 1944 we were scrambled from Salzwedel against the Viermots. In the area of Frankfurt–Limburg–Siegen–Giessen we got contact with the enemy. The bombers were well protected by Mustangs and therefore it was of paramount importance to engage the bombers in a swift surprise attack. We succeeded by turning in to the bombers sooner than expected. I swung in 400–500m [437–547 yards] behind a bomber and was at once met by intense defensive fire.

"At the same time I kept an eye on a Mustang which approached me, firing its guns. He was about 300m [328 yards] away and I thought he would never hit me at this turning speed. Apart from that, I was certain that he would break off his attack in order not to expose himself to the fire of his own bombers. But I was mistaken. While firing at the bomber with all my guns, I was suddenly hit from behind. At the same time there was a dull bang which shook my Fw 190A-8. In no time at all, the cockpit windows were completely covered in oil and I could see nothing. I tried to jettison the cockpit cover, but without success. It had opened only halfway which made bailing out impossible. Meanwhile, flames were licking along the fuselage. I threw my machine into a steep left turn and let the aircraft slip away to the inside. The flames were thus forced away from the fuselage and later on went out. I made an emergency landing in the vicinity of Dornholzhausen/Bad Homburg in the Taunus."

a short leave, the *Gruppe* had been transferred. Our new airfield was Schafhof near Amberg, I flew several sorties from here, frequently together with Gefreiter, later Unteroffizier Eugen Meier. He was a good chum, tough and full of energy.

"During a sortie around Creilsheim we got into contact with Mustangs. We had a tough dogfight, Eugen shot down one Mustang and I two. Then I was again hanging on my parachute. I got a good reception by an army unit who confirmed our successes. Dogfights with Mustangs and Thunderbolts were for us flying the Me 109 a question of altitude, we were about even up to 6–8,000m [6,562–8,749 yards], at higher altitudes only with extra fuel injection which one could not use for very long. The 109 was hard on the controls, but after being used to flying the Me 110 and 410, not too much so."

Left: Some 6,845 Purple Hearts were made to 8th Air Force combat airmen from August 17, 1942 to May 15, 1945.

Below: Pilots of 4th Staffel, Jagdgeschwader (JG) 1 at Woensdrecht trying to relax in deckchairs during Bereitschaff (readiness) alongside a Fw 190A-5.

Unteroffizier Walter Ibold, Bf 109 pilot, 2./JG 26, who in late fall 1944 was posted to 14./JG 300, still flying the Bf 109G, recalled: "From 23 July till 17 October 1944 I was with the 2nd Staffel of JG 76. I flew 10 or 12 sorties, all with enemy contact and claimed two Mustangs shot down around Recklinghausen. When I returned after four weeks in hospital and

Feldwebel Horst Petzschler, a Bf 109G-6 pilot in I./JG 3 "Udet," shot down a B-17 at Frankfurt am Main and a Mustang southeast of Frankfurt—his fourth and fifth victories. "When a 'pearl string' of five Mustangs came down on me from high up and from the northeast, there was only one thing to do and to head face-to-face with the first one and

next was literally flying for my life, I was chased down from 24,000ft [7,315m] to ground level by four P-51s. Out-climbing them was out of the question as I was running out of fuel! When the warning light indicates the fuel running out, one is additionally nervous. Hedge-hopping to the northeast, I drew the Mustangs into 2cm quadruple flak fire from Fritzlar airfield in Thuringia. I swiftly carried out an emergency landing, but since I had been hit several times, the landing ended in a spin around as one of my undercarriage legs broke off! Luckily, the P-51s were brushed off by a great and very alert flak crew."

On Sunday May 28, 1944, I./JG 3 lost four Bf 109G-6s and two pilots killed in combat with the Mustang escorts in the Magdeburg area. Feldwebel Horst Petzschler, who led the *Staffel*, recalled: "When the bomber stream came in to attack Magdeburg/Kassel we were in position above the Fw 190 *Sturmgruppe* that mercilessly started attacking the B-17 boxes from head-on. We were safe from the flak at our height of 30,000ft [9,144m], but P-51D Mustangs attacked us from higher up than 30,000ft! My wingman went down first ... but the attacking P-51D was passing me fast, I could give him a good burst of my weapons and he went down ... Meanwhile our whole Staffel was split up and single dogfights developed, although we were strictly forbidden to engage in it, as we had to concentrate on destroying the bombers... Another P-51D hacked a third of my left wing off and made my machine unflyable, so I bailed out."

Above: *Kommodore Oberstleutnant Hans Philipp and several officers of III./Gruppe, JG 1. Philipp was shot down and killed by US fighters on October 8, 1943 flying an Fw 190A-6.*

Above top: *German FuG 7 aircraft radio used in the Messerschmitt Bf 109G-2 fighter on display in the Finnish Air Force Signals Museum.*

Right: *On April 16, 1944, Major Schnoor, Kommandeur 1./JG 1 had a narrow escape when his Fw 190A-7 "White 20" touched trees in low-level flight and crashed as a result.*

giving a lot of deflection, about five-plane lengths. My luck was to hit the P-51 first and we passed each other closely. Coming in and around to be ready for the other four, I saw my adversary explode in a large fireball! My underwear was already wet, but what came

Bandits and Targets

On September 17, 1944, 1,113 medium and heavy bombers escorted by 330 fighter aircraft carried out bombing attacks to eliminate the opposition before the airborne forces of Operation *Market Garden* went in later that day. The 4th and 361st Fighter Groups were among those who tussled with JG 26 in the mid-afternoon on this momentous day. For four pilots killed in action, JG 26 claimed three of the yellow-jackets in the Mönchengladbach and Nijmegen areas and two 4th Fighter Group P-51s in the Emmerich–Bocholt area. The 4th Fighter Group was led by the CO, Lieutenant Colonel Kinnard, when fifteen Focke-Wulfs bounced a few P-51s in the 335th Squadron. Leutnant Wilhelm Hofmann and Oberfähnrich Gerhard "Bubi" Schulwitz shot down two of the P-51s. Captain Louis H. "Red Dog" Norley got on the tail of one Fw 190 and claimed it as destroyed and 1st Lieutenant Ted E. Lines claimed three Fw 190s to put him on seven enemy aircraft destroyed in two missions. Lines reported: "…when we were bounced from behind and above by 15 Fw 190s…my wingman hollered for me to break as I was trying to discard my

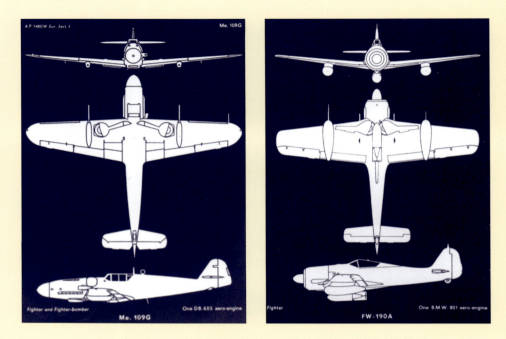

Above: *Messerschmitt Bf 109G (left) and Focke-Wulf 190A (right) silhouettes used for aircraft recognition by US pilots.*

right external wing tank. When I broke, I was head-on to five Fw 190s and immediately started firing, causing one Fw 190 to burst into flames. I turned starboard, still trying to drop my tank, as two Fws came under me, heading in the same direction as I was. I got on the tail of the one nearest me and started firing and the pilot bailed out. At this point, a 190 closed on my tail and fired at me, hitting me in the tail and wing. My tank finally came off and I was able to maneuver onto the tail of the 190 that had

Above right: *The 357th Fighter Group's top four aces are seen together at Yoxford in Suffolk during the autumn of 1944: Captain Richard Allen "Bud" Peterson (left); Major "Kit" Carson (2nd from left); Major John England (2nd from right); Captain Clarence Emil "Bud" Anderson.*

Above left: *P-51D 44-13887 "Little Joe" in the 36rd FS, 357th FG, at Leiston with ground crew. Ground mechanics wore the D-1 jacket and B-1 trousers, in use from 1940 and similar in design to the winter flying B-6 jacket and A-3 trousers.*

been firing at me. After three orbits, he broke for the deck with me right on his tail. I fired from 500 yards [457m] down to about 100 yards [91m] and saw strikes on his engine, canopy, fuselage, wings and tail. He burst into flames and went into the ground and exploded."

Right and below: Captain Yeager in the 363rd FS, 357th FG, with his ground crew at Leiston, Suffolk in front of "Glamorous Glen" (below).

up, found my wingman, assembled the squadron over Wesel and completed our mission."

On November 6, Captain "Chuck" Yeager in the 357th Fighter Group, who had become separated, found himself near a large airfield: "I spotted a lone '262 approaching the field from the south at 500ft [152m]. He was going very slow (about 200mph [322kmph]), I split-S'ed on it and was going around 500mph [805kmph] at 500ft [152m]. Flak started coming up very thick and accurate. I fired a single short burst from around 400 yards [366m] and got hits on the wings. I had to break straight up and looking back, saw the jet enemy aircraft crash-land about 400 yards [366m] short of the field... a wing flew off outside the right jet unit. The plane did not burn." **He was credited with the destruction of the Me 262 and two others "damaged."**

Yeager finished the war with 11.5 aerial victories, including five Bf 109s on October 12 and four Fw 190s on November 27, 1944. On October 12, Yeager was flying *Glamorous Glennis* **(named after his future wife):** "They did not see us coming at them out of the sun... I came in behind their tail-end Charlie ... when he suddenly broke left and ran into his wingman. They both bailed out. It was almost comic, scoring two quick victories without firing a shot. By now all the airplanes in the sky had dropped their tanks and were spinning and diving in a wild, wide-open dogfight. I blew up a 109 from 600 yards [549m]—my third victory—when I turned around and saw another angling in behind me. Man, I pulled back on my throttle so damned hard I nearly stalled, rolled up and over, came in behind and under him, kicking right rudder and simultaneously firing. I was directly underneath the guy, less than 50ft [15m] and I opened up that 109 as if it were a can of Spam. That made four. A moment later I waxed a guy's fanny in a steep dive. I pulled up at about 1,000ft [305m]; he went straight into the ground." **Yeager loved to dogfight. "It was a clean contest of skill, stamina and courage; one on one." He went on to gain immortal fame when he officially became the first pilot to break the sound barrier on December 12, 1953, flying the Bell X-1A.**

In his combat report, Captain Louis H. Norley stated: "The bandits had been flying at the base of a layer of haze and with their light gray color were very difficult to see… I dropped my tanks. In a port break, I met an aircraft head-on firing at me. These were supposedly 109s and this one, with an inline engine; looked like an enemy. I fired a short burst at long range. I then noticed two 190s on his tail; the closest one firing and getting strikes, as it became apparent that the plane I fired on was a P-51. I broke up, coming down on the tail of the 190 as he broke off his attack and turned to port. I dropped 20° of flaps and turned with him, the other 190 being attacked by my wingman. I fired. The 190 rolled and started to split-S, but leveled out and started to climb. I fired again with no results.

"He leveled off and did some skidding evasion efforts as I closed firing and skidding past him. He dove to port, allowing me to drop back on his tail. I fired, getting many strikes on his wings and fuselage. He flicked over on his back. The canopy and some pieces flew off and he went into a vertical dive, crashing into a farmyard where the plane blew up… I climbed

Great Day For The Yellow Jackets

On September 27, 1944, when 315 Liberators went to the Henschel engine and vehicle assembly plants at Kassel in central Germany, the 445th Bomb Group flew into an area a few miles from Eisenach where II./JG 4, IV./JG 3 "Udet," and II./JG 300, each with a strength of around thirty specially configured Fw 190s with heavy armor plate, were forming for an attack. In less than ten minutes the *Sturmgruppen* attacks downed twenty-five Liberators. B-24 pilots put out frantic calls for help on the fighter channel and immediately two Mustang groups covering the 3rd Division, 75 miles (121km) away near Frankfurt, and the 361st Fighter Group, escorting the 1st Division 100 miles (161km) distant, were speeding to the rescue. Six precious minutes were to elapse before the 361st Fighter Group could reach the beleaguered 445th Bomb Group and the other two P-51 groups arrived after the enemy had departed.

Unteroffizier Ernst Schröder, a *Sturmfighter* in II. Sturm/JG 300, who had been born in Cologne, took off from Finsterwalde in his Fw 190A-8 "Red 19" *Kolle-alaaf* [Cologne Aloft] with the rest of his *Gruppe*. Schröder shot down two of the B-24s. There was so much debris in the sky that he closed his eyes because he believed he would run into something. Ten to 15 columns of smoke from the explosions of the crashing aircraft rose up through the cloud layer about 3,280ft (1,000m) above the ground. There was burning wreckage everywhere and the fields were covered with white parachutes. At almost 328ft (100m) above the ground, Schröder could clearly see crewmen who had bailed out running through the fields.

"When I flew over they stood and raised their hands high. Soldiers and policemen were running towards them to take them captive. Suddenly a P-51B with a yellow nose shot towards me. In the wink of an eye we raced closely by each other on an opposite course. When we had flown by one another, the maneuver began anew, so that we flew towards one another like jousting knights of the Middle Ages. Both of us opened fire simultaneously. The American hit my tail section. My two heavy MG 131 30mm cannon and MG 151/20 20mm guns failed after a few shots.

"Since I could not fire a shot I began evasive maneuvers the moment the American opened fire, so that he could not aim correctly. It was a strange feeling each time looking into the flash of his four 12.7mm guns. After we had played this little game five or six times I escaped by flying low over the

Above and right: P-51D 44-13926 E2-S being flown by 1st Lieutenant Urban Drew in the 375th Fighter Squadron. Drew finished his combat tour with six confirmed victories. In May 1983, he was presented with the Air Force Cross.

ground. The American turned sharply but the camouflage paint on my Fw 190 made it difficult for him to find me against the dappled ground. I landed after minutes of fearful sweating at Langen-sala after 90 minutes of flight time. An inspection showed some hits in the tail section and a part of the covering of my rudder was torn off but the damage was so slight that I could take off again at noon. This event made it very clear that the Americans in 1944 had air superiority only because their fighter escorts were very effective and often they were successful in protecting the bombers against German fighters."

In a brief battle 361st Fighter Group Mustangs shot down a few enemy fighters. 2nd Lieutenant Leo H. Lamb of Blue Flight was killed when his P-51B was apparently rammed by a German fighter. 1st Lieutenant Victor Bocquin claimed three Fw 190s destroyed while 1st Lieutenant William "Bill" Rockafeller Beyer claimed five. Credited with a total of eighteen German aircraft destroyed in the air and another three on the ground, the 376th Squadron had set a temporary record among the fighter groups of the 8th Air Force for enemy aircraft destroyed by a single squadron on a single mission.

Lieutenant Urban L. Drew made history on October 7, when he single-handedly bounced a pair of Me 262s as they took off from Achmer, destroying both. On this mission he was leading the 375th Fighter Squadron as escort to B-17s attacking targets in Czechoslovakia. On the return flight he kept a careful watch for jets as they neared Osnabrück and was rewarded as they passed close to

Above: Close finger fours, echeloned down from the lead flight, were flown so there was no excuse for losing formation.

Right: Pilot Gefreiter Ernst Schroeder, II.Sturm/JG 300 in his Fw 190 "Red 19' Kolle-alaaf!" (Cologne aloft).

the jet base at Achmer. Two aircraft were taxiing out. He called his deputy squadron leader, Captain Bruce Rowlett, to take over. Urban Drew remembers: "Waited until both airborne, then rolled over from 15,000ft [4,572m] with my flight following and caught up with second Me 262 when he was 1,000ft [914m] off the ground. I was indicating 450mph [724kmph]. The Me 262 couldn't have been going over 200mph [322kmph]. I started firing from approximately 400 yards [366m], 30° deflection and, as I closed, I saw hits all over the wings and fuselage. Just as I passed him I saw a sheet of flame come out from near the right wing root and as I glanced back I saw a gigantic explosion and a sheet of red flame over area of 1,000ft [914m].

"The other Me 262 was 500 yards [457m] ahead and had started a fast climbing turn to the left. I was still indicating 440mph [708kmph] and had to haul back to stay with him. I started shooting from about 60° deflection, and just hitting his tail section. I kept horsing back and hits crept up his fuselage to his cockpit. Just after that I saw his canopy fly off in two sections, his plane roll over and go into a flat spin. He then hit the ground on his back at 60° angle and exploded violently. I did not see the pilot bail out. Two huge columns of smoke came up from both Me 262s burning on the ground."

Leutnant Gerhard Kobert was killed when his Messerschmitt blew up and Hauptmann Arnold was flying the second Me 262. Urban Drew insists that the pilot could not have survived.

Left: Mechanics work on the engine of a 361st Fighter Group Mustang at Bottisham airfield, UK.

"Ace Van"

"Sandy—this is 'ACE' Van, and I really mean it. I got one and a half planes today. That gives me five and one-half... We were cruising along and spotted ten Fw 190s and bounced them... My regards to all. 'ACE VAN'"

—From 1st Lieutenant George R. Vanden Heuvel's letter to his brother

On December 26, 1944, fourteen Mustangs in the 361st Fighter Group flew their first mission from St. Dizier with a sweep near Trier Göttingen at 17,000ft [5,181m]. Ten-plus Fw 190D-9 "Doras" led by Oberleutnant Hans Hartigs of the 4th Staffel, Jagdgeschwader 26, passed in front of the P-51s on a perpendicular course, momentarily unaware of the Americans. The 376th Fighter Squadron executed a diving turn to catch the German formation from behind. George Vanden Heuvel flying Yorkshire Red Four (tail-end Charlie) in *Mary Mine* recalled: "We turned on them and they broke into us. Lieutenant Claire P. Chennault turned onto one and another turned toward him. I got on the Fw's tail and he headed for the deck in a series of steep diving turns. I shot short bursts at him from about 300 yards [273m] on the way down, registering occasional hits. He levelled off at about 100ft [32m] and started a turn to the right. I set the K-14 gunsight on him and fired a long burst, opening fire at 250 yards [228m], 20 degree deflection. Closing to 200 yards [182m], I registered numerous hits on his fuselage, canopy and wing roots. He fell off on one wing and dove into the ground, exploding upon impact. The pilot did not bail out. I then took a picture of the wreck.

Above and left: Operating from St. Dizier, France, on December 26, 1944, 1st Lieutenant George R. Vanden Heuvel (above) in the 376th Fighter Squadron, 361st Fighter Group, shot down an Fw 190D-9 flown by Luftwaffe ace Oberleutnant Hans Hartigs of the 4th Staffel, JG 26, seen here on the left. Hartigs spent the rest of the war in captivity.

"I started climbing up and about 5 miles [8km] east of me I saw two planes on the deck. I finally identified them as a Fw 190 being chased by Captain Jay Ruch. I told him I was covering him and he said he was out of ammunition and for me to shoot the Fw 190 down.

The Fw 190 was smoking slightly and taking weak evasive action on the deck. As he pulled up out of a gully, I clobbered him from about 300 yards [273m], 15 degrees deflection, firing several bursts. He started a turn to the left and I clobbered him again from 200 yards [182m] and several pieces flew off the plane. He rolled over on his back and bailed out."

Vanden Heuvel claimed an Fw 190 destroyed and one shared with Captain Jay Ruch. After landing from the mission Lieutenant Jack Mitenbuler in the 374th Fighter Squadron had been compelled to land at an airfield due to battle damage. He met a German pilot captured by US ground forces after bailing out of his Fw 190 after being shot up by two "yellow nosed Mustangs." It was Hartigs, who had been flying for about seven years with the Luftwaffe. After his Dora half-rolled Hartigs had bailed out when his oil pressure dropped and his canopy filmed over with oil. Vanden Heuvel noticed that he was wearing a "beautiful leather outfit trimmed in white." When Hartigs hit the ground he could see the dead body of one of his 4th Staffel pilots lying on a parachute. A GI had shot Unteroffizier Hermann Grad at close range. Hartigs' life was spared and he was marched off to captivity. In all, six "Doras" were claimed shot down (five were actually lost) without loss.

Right: Crew chiefs watch as a 361st Fighter Group Mustang comes into land.

Below: Oberleutnant Waldemar "Waldi" Radener in his Fw 190 A-8 "Brown 4" (W.Nr. 340001) leading 7./JG 26 from Coesfeld-Stevede on May 4, 1944. Note the rows of victory bars on the rudder of Radener's aircraft.

Fated Never To Fly Again

At Altenburg on November 2, 1944, twenty-year old Helmut Peter Rix began his conversion onto the Focke-Wulf Fw 190: "After three flights in a two-seat Fw 190A-8/U1, I went solo while carrying out circuits; we were limited to five take-offs and landing each day under normal circumstances. We continued fighter training over the firing range and made close formation flights in twos and fours at altitudes up to 30,000ft [9,144m]. In mid-December we moved again, to Neustadt/Glewe to join I Staffel of the operational training unit 1./JG 2 *Erganzungs Geschwader* for more intensive combat training, which took in high-altitude flying with the entire *Staffel* and dogfighting. We did not stay long and on January 12, 1945, I was posted to 8 Staffel II./JG 301 at Welzow. My fellow pilots and I hardly had time to get acquainted before the 'scramble' order came through—eight out of ten of my new comrades did not return! The American fighter-bombers, P-51s and P-38s, were masters of the air.

"On March 2 elements of *Geschwader* JG 301 scrambled at 10:15 hours to intercept 8th Air Force heavy bombers and their escort. I walked out to my aircraft, Fw 190D-9, 'Red 4' part of a *Schwarm* led by the Staffelkapitän, Leutnant Walter Kropp. It was a beautiful morning, clear

Above left: Various German aircraft lie destroyed at the airbases.
Above right: The remains of Major "Kit" Carson's P-51K-5 44-11622 "Nooky Booky IV" in a German scrap yard near Nuremberg in the summer of 1945.

Above top: 2nd Lieutenant John W. Gokey's USAAF Aviator's Flight Bag, previously owned by Lieutenant C. J. Slonneger. The flight bag was used to carry personal effects and clothing.

blue sky, but with a cloud cover of 8/10ths at about 14,000ft [4,267m]. I climbed on a southeast course to 24,000ft [7,315m] when we spotted our target, a formation of B-17s at 27,000ft [8,230m] dead ahead. We were in line-abreast formation and ready for a frontal attack when Kropp broke away to the left into a dive. Doing so, we got into a line-astern formation with me as No. 4. The lead aircraft was disappearing into the clouds when my plane shuddered and flames were licking around the front of the engine."

Rix's Fw 190 was destroyed by gunfire from Captain Lee Kilgo and Lieutenant Earl Mundell of the 486th Squadron, 352nd Fighter Group, which claimed 5.5 victories over the 190s. Kilgo, in his encounter report, stated: "I was flying No. 4 in Yellow flight when the flight engaged one Fw 190 and began a Lufbery [maneuver]. The e/a [enemy aircraft] turned away, placing me in position on his tail. At long range I fired several bursts and he began smoking and went into a turning dive directly over a town. I broke away—the flight leader saw him crash in flames."

Mundell reported: "My flight was higher, thereby giving me a better chance to close on him. I was making good progress when two P-51s came in from the side. One ship got several hits. The 190 threw out some smoke and broke right and down to an altitude of 15,000ft [4,572m] . I tacked on, fired a long burst—some parts flew off and the pilot bailed out near 8,000ft [2,438m]. The ship hit and exploded not far from a small town."

All four Fw 190s were shot down during this battle, with Helmut Rix the only survivor. "In the panic that followed I got rid of my cockpit hood but forgot to undo my straps first and so fed the flames with the aircraft out of control. I managed to undo the straps but how I got out I shall never know. My 'chute opened perfectly. As I drifted down I realized that the fire had caused severe burns to my head, face, and lower arms. By the time I landed in about six inches of snow, I was nearly blinded and was dragged along by my parachute for some distance. I was then picked up by a local farmer and taken to hospital in Aussig in the German Sudetenland. There is little doubt that wearing a full leather combination flying suit had saved my life.

"After seven weeks and transfer to another hospital in Comotou I discharged myself because things were getting rather hot with the Russians too close for comfort. Besides, I wanted to rejoin my *Staffel*. It was a dreadful journey through a burning Aussig and Dresden and on to Berlin. I had to dodge Russian shells landing around the Bahnhof Friederichstrasse, from where I made my exit to Staaken on the western outskirts of Berlin. I looked a mess, with my head and arms still bandaged and my leathers burned. When I reached the airfield control tower, the CO greeted me as if I were a ghost!

"I found out where my *Staffel* was located and arranged transport on a convoy heading northwest that same night. It proved to be another precarious trip but we arrived unscathed at Neustadt Glewe, where I was re-united with 8. Staffel. They were equally surprised to see me—I had been posted as 'missing' and nobody knew what fate had befallen me. I found out we had been attacked by Mustangs just as we were diving into the clouds. I was fated never to fly again, no matter how hard I tried to persuade the medics. It broke my heart to see my comrades take off for fighter-bomber attacks in Berlin and, on many occasions, fail to return. The Russians advanced further and further and in the end the entire strength of JG 301 moved northwest to Heidi in Schleswig-Holstein and to Leck. There we were taken over by 2nd Tactical Air Force and interned with the individual *Staffeln* bivouacking on farms until they were disbanded.

"So ended my career, shattered into nothing. In the aftermath of the war it took me a long, long time to pick myself up and start my life over again. But at least I had over 250 hours flying time and my life had been enriched by the experience."

The American Flying Jacket

The American A-2 flying jacket was adopted by the US Army Air Corps in 1931, and it became a signature piece of dress for US air personnel throughout World War II. Officially described as "Jacket, Flying, Type A-2," the jacket featured a snap-flap pocket of each side, knit cuffs and waistband, a snap-down collar, shoulder straps, and a zipper fastening at the front. The latter was made from steel or brass, and nickel-plated varieties are also seen.

Above: 2nd Lieutenant John W. Gokey's A-2 jacket. Gokey, in the 503rd FS in the 339th FG at Fowlmere near Duxford in Cambridgeshire, was wearing it on Monday 11, December 1944 when he suffered engine failure and he bailed out before his Mustang crashed in the back garden of a house in Frinton-on-Sea, Essex.

End Game

"I closed to about 400 yards [366m] on an Fw 190 at the rear of a gaggle, firing a good burst and getting strikes all over his fuselage. I believe the pilot was killed. I went back up to the bombers, looked around for a couple of minutes and saw a formation of about forty to fifty Fw 190s coming up about 1,000 yards [914m] behind."

—Captain Leonard Kyle "Kit" Carson, who on November 27, 1944, shot down five Fw 190s

On Christmas Eve 1944, a record 2,034 8th Air Force Liberators and B-17s took part in the largest single strike flown by the Allied air forces in World War II, in support of the Allied armies in the Ardennes. At about 09:00 hours on New Year's Day 1945, *Unternehmen Bodenplatte* (Operation *Baseplate*)—a desperate gamble to diminish the overwhelming Allied air superiority—was launched by the Luftwaffe with the aim of delivering a single, decisive blow against RAF and American aircraft on the ground in Holland, Belgium, and northern France using 875 single-engined fighter aircraft, primarily in support of von Rundstedt's Ardennes offensive. The outcome, though, was far different. Though total Allied aircraft losses during *Bodenplatte* amounted to 424 destroyed or heavily damaged, the Luftwaffe losses were catastrophic; 300 aircraft were lost, 235 pilots were killed and sixty-five pilots were taken prisoner. The big gamble turned into a disastrous defeat.

German jet fighters had made a few concerted attempts at turning back the bombers late in 1944, but on each occasion they had been beaten off with heavy losses inflicted by escorting P-51 Mustangs and P-47 Thunderbolts of the 8th Air Force. The Junkers Jumo 004B-2 axial-flow turbojet unit fitted to the Me 262 was

Left: P-51D in the colors of 44-13704 B7-H "Ferocious Frankie," which was flown by Lieutenant Colonel Wallace E. Hopkins in the 361st FG at Bottisham, his second Mustang named for his wife.

supposed to last from 25 to 35 hours, but in practice they lasted only about ten hours' flying time. Despite the jet's speed and performance at altitude, the Germans recognized that the Me 262 was not invincible. Its fuel consumption was enormous and that limited its range and endurance. It was particularly vulnerable during takeoff and landing. Allied fighter pilots made full use of this. Fortunately, the German jets and V-weapons had materialized far too late and in too few numbers to alter the outcome of the war.

On January 14, 1945, the red and yellow-nosed P-51s of the 357th Fighter Group at Leiston, Suffolk, shot down 60.5 enemy aircraft in a single day; a record for any 8th Air Force fighter group that still stood by the end of hostilities in Europe. The 20th Fighter Group claimed 19.5 victories and the 353rd Fighter Group claimed nine enemy aircraft shot down. In all, 161 enemy aircraft were destroyed. In the previous eleven months the veteran 357th Fighter Group's pilots had been credited with 517 victories. No fewer than thirty-nine pilots had attained ace status.

By 14:45 hours on January 14 all the 357th Fighter Group Mustangs had landed and pilots were soon telling their mission accounts to amazed interrogation officers. Only thirteen P-51s and three P-47 Thunderbolts were lost during the air battle. The 357th Fighter Group was awarded a Distinguished Unit Citation (DUC) for its outstanding performance.

Saturday Night

When 1st Lieutenant Walter J. Konantz flew a freelance area support mission on January 13, 1945, it was a day he would remember for the rest of his life. He not only recorded his third kill, but it was the first claim for a Me 262 jet by the 55th Fighter Group. Konantz recalls: "We were trimmed down from the usual 50 or so planes to just 37 P-51s. The 338th Squadron had three flights totaling 12 planes. The three squadrons spread out for a search for targets of opportunity. The 338th, having destroyed 14 planes on the ground at Giebelstadt airfield just a week before, headed for this field to see if there were any left. The dozen Mustangs were circling the field at about 5,000ft [1,524m], planning our strafing routes and picking out targets on the ground.

"At this point I saw a plane taxiing onto the runway and was surprised to see him take off. I would have thought we had been seen and the tower would have advised him to park the plane and seek shelter. I called out the now airborne plane but no one else saw him. He continued climbing; made a 180° turn and came back directly under me headed in the opposite direction. I did a tight 180 and ended up about 200 yards [183m] behind him.

"At this point, he had built up enough speed that I was no longer closing on him, even though I was at full throttle and had made a diving turn behind him. The new K-14 gyroscopic gunsight had been installed in this plane only a week earlier and I had never fired the guns with this new sight before. It worked perfectly and the German plane, now identified as a Me 262, was saturated with nearly 40 hits. He made no evasive action whatsoever, possibly the pilot may have been hit. His left engine burst into flame and the Me 262 made a slow descending spiral and crashed on a railroad track about 2 miles (3.2km] from the airfield.

Left: A P-51 model carved out of Perspex from the Mustang's bubble canopy.

Below: 1st Lt Walter Konantz (left) with his pet dog "Scottie" and his younger brother, 2nd Lt Harold Konantz (right) both of the 338th FS, 55th FG.

The plane exploded on impact and probably cut the track." **The pilot of the Me 262 (Werk Nu. 110601 9K+EH) was Unteroffizier Alfred Färber of 1./KGJ 51, another former bomber unit that was converting to the jet aircraft at Giebelstadt. Färber was on an acceptance flight following maintenance and repair work on his Me 262.**

On January 29, 1945, Konantz notched his fourth aerial victory of the war when the 55th Fighter Group escorted the B-17s to Kassel. He wrote. "Two flights (eight P-51s) left the bombers for a fighter sweep on the way out. Our flight ran into three Me 109s at about 5,000ft [1,524m], 100 miles [161km] northwest of Hamburg. I saw them first and led the flight to them. I picked the leader who was carrying an external belly tank. The other two were clean. I got a good burst into him, setting his belly tank on fire. He promptly dropped it and continued on, leading me over a small town that was throwing up 20mm flak. We ended up over the town at about 50ft [15m], circling a brewery smokestack below its top. We were in a hard right turn pulling three or four Gs when I got a hit on his left aileron, blowing about a third of it off. The sudden loss of lift on that side caused him to violently snap to an inverted position. I left my gun camera running, expecting him to split-S into the middle of the town but he climbed inverted to a safe altitude and rolled upright.

"He then headed out into open country flying so low he was pulling up over fences and descending again on the other side. His prop tips were barely clearing the snow-covered ground and his prop wash was blowing up snow behind him like a car on a dusty road. After another good burst of hits, he simply pushed forward on the stick and bellied in at 280mph [386kmph]. He slid for more than a half mile, coming to rest in a grove of

Left: *Me 262 seen through the K-14A gunsight of a P-51D.*

Below: *Lockheed P-38 Lightning carved out of aircraft Perspex; such carvings were popularly used as ornaments, trinkets, or brooches; the latter as a gift for English girlfriends and small boys.*

trees with his wings sheared off. When I passed over him, he was climbing out of the cockpit and saluted me as I went by. My wingman was close behind me and strafed the wreckage, setting it on fire. Whether or not the pilot escaped the strafing, neither my wingman nor me knew. **Forty-nine years later Walt Konantz learned that the fighter was a Bf 109G-14 "Blue 32" and that it was being flown by Oberleutnant Waldemar Balasus of II./JG 27.**

On February 23, Walt Konantz flew his sixty-fourth and final fighter mission in Mustang *Saturday Night*. He recorded in his log: "Escorted B-17s to Nurnberg—led Red Flight. After escorting bombers a safe distance out I went back in with my flight, searching desperately for one more enemy aircraft as this was my last mission and I had only four."

Saturday Night was taken over by 2nd Lieutenant Harold Konantz, his younger brother, who had just arrived as a replacement pilot. The P-51 earned a Bronze Star for its crew chief Staff Sergeant James Seibert, by flying over sixty combat missions without a mechanical abort. Harold Konantz left the name on the nose and had only to change the rank and first name on the canopy tail. On April 7, 1945, he was flying his seventh mission when he was hit by gunfire from a B-17 waist gunner 50 miles [80km] northwest of Berlin. Harold lost his coolant and the engine caught fire forcing a bail-out. He was a PoW for the rest of the war.

Following Walt Konantz's experience, fifteen more Me 262 jets would fall to 55th Fighter Group pilots before the end of hostilities in Europe.

Home To Mother England

On March 19, 1945, Mustangs flew 606 effective sorties in support of the bombers, and over one hundred enemy fighters including thirty-six jets in formation (the largest number yet seen in one formation) were encountered. US fighters claimed forty-two enemy fighters (including three jets) destroyed. Major Robin Olds of the **434th Fighter Squadron, 479th Fighter Group in his P-51K, claimed a Bf 109 and an Fw 190 to take his score to twelve victories.**

1st Lieutenant Richard G. Simpson confirmed the Fw 190D-9 that Major Olds claimed: "Upon encountering the enemy aircraft we climbed to about 13,000ft [3,962m] and joined in their Lufbery to the left. Red Flight was directly behind White Flight and as the Lufbery got tighter, I saw a 109 roll over on his back, skid and then spin violently down. I did not see whether this 109 was under attack or not because of the haze and contrails. Nor did I see any strikes. The German leader was getting uncomfortably close in the turn, so I gave the word to break into them. Because of the contrails and haze, I continued the Lufbery, not knowing whether the Jerries were on our tails or not.

"A few moments later Major Olds ordered us to get below the contrail level; so I split-S'ed, pulling out at about 8,000ft [2,438m]. As I leveled off I saw a Fw 190 with two P-51s on his tail. The 190 was smoking badly and then he rolled over and went down in a steep dive, losing pieces of cowling and other parts as they flew off his aircraft. I broke to the right with my flight in order to investigate two bogeys, which turned out to be a P-51 attacking another 190. The 190 pulled up sharply and I saw the P-51 firing and getting strikes all over the Jerry's fuselage."

Above center: Badge of the "Mighty Eighth" Air Force.

Right: Fw 190A-4 in the markings of the Technical Officer of II, Gruppe JG 1 with his personal emblem and Tatzelwurm motif. The Fw 190 was one of the finest single-seat fighters produced by Germany during World War II. The A-4 variant was introduced in July 1942.

Olds destroyed a Bf 109 over the Dummer Lake on April 7 and he also damaged a Me 262, to take his score to thirteen victories. He was also credited with four MiG-21s shot down in combat during the Vietnam War in January–May 1967.

On March 3, 1945, Marvin C. Bigelow in the 78th Fighter Group had an encounter with an Me 262: "The penetration was to be a deep one into Germany. When I saw my mount I could hardly believe it. The modifications to this aircraft were amazing. To begin with it was basically a P-51B, which was an early model to say the least. At one time the ship had been equipped with dive brakes, which had been welded shut. The razorback had been modified with a Malcolm hood that gave more room and better visibility but with a certain amount of visual distortion. This war-weary bird still carried grey paint—at least where it hadn't worn through or been chipped off—and undoubtedly had had numerous engine changes. On the other side of the ledger, she was modified to carry external tanks and had the usual number of 50 calibers. The clouds were high and it was a beautiful day to travel.

"We picked up the bomber stream on schedule and at 22,000ft [6,705m] flew down the stream looking for our assigned group. There was a veritable river of aircraft headed east and all pulling contrails. I understand this was done purposely in order to let those below know the hopelessness of their situation. We found the group and began our work, 'S' turning across our 'Big Friends' in order to prevent their being surprised.

"On a sweeping turn to the left the entire canopy suddenly frosted over, making a quick shift to instruments necessary. I pushed the mike button, gave the reason, and said I was dropping out of formation. A mid-air collision was not a happy thought and could have led to serious injury.

"It was customary under these circumstances to leave in pairs, but then the canopy cleared at 18,000ft [5,486m] and I could see the outside

Below: P-51D-20 44-63864 "Twilight Tear" in the famous colors of the 78th Fighter Group landing at Duxford in 2002. From January 1945, "Twilight Tear" was flown at Duxford by Lieutenant Hubert "Bill" Davis, who named his aircraft after a horse.

Left: The 9th Air Force was established in late 1942, and from 1943 to 1945 it served as the tactical arm of the USAAF in Western Europe. The 9th Air Force badge is here seen with a US service plaque.

"Ten minutes later I saw a stream of four boxes of B-17s headed south, dead ahead and about 2,000ft [610m] above me. Reaching the conclusion there would be safety in numbers I started to climb to become their escort, which they apparently lacked. I soon noticed an element of aircraft fast approaching the bombers from the rear. When the lead ship of the element dove through the boxed bombers firing, about six shells from each of his wing cannon, I started to cut him off in a dive.

"When I had him in the K-14, the Me 262 was no more than half an inch. A glance at the airspeed showed an indicated 650mph [1,046kmph] at 17,000ft [5,182m]. The jet had shrunk to about a quarter inch when a second glance showed 680mph [1,094 kmph] and the Mustang finally began to complain. She was shaking herself like a wet puppy. The jet was gone completely, at what speed I could only guess as I was alone in the sky and down

world, the bomber stream, contrails and my safety escort were nowhere to be seen. I was by myself and terribly lonesome. As I swiveled my neck trying to look in all directions at once, the only 'familiar' sign I saw was Dummer Lake, a checkpoint used on many missions. This was no place for a small, lonesome boy so I decided to go home to Mother England and took the correct heading.

to 10,000ft [3,048m]. I headed back to England and the mission whiskey.

"Later looking back at the circumstances I couldn't help wondering why or by what quirk of fate, I, who was on the winning side, would be flying that war-weary bird while my opponent who left the scene, did so in an obviously vastly superior aircraft. That was the last mission for the Mustang I rode that day."

Jet-Feast

On the mission to Magdeburg on January 16, 1945, Jockey Blue flight in the 353rd Fighter Group was led by Captain Glenn G. Callans, who had a successful day when they attacked Deiningen landing ground. Callans recalled: "We were approximately 10 minutes ahead of our big friends along the withdrawal route. I spotted a satellite landing ground to the left of our briefed route. There were approximately 15 to 20 enemy aircraft dispersed on the west and northwest side of the field. I called for a line abreast formation at 8,000ft [2,438m] and then we started down west of the field from up-sun. I started firing at a Ju 88 at 500 yards [457m] and continued to fire to point blank range, scoring many hits in the cockpit area, but no fires were noted. Flak was very light and inaccurate.

"I noted an Me 163 being serviced in front of a hanger, so I started a tight turn to the left and proceeded to make another pass at this aircraft. I approached the field from the southwest to the northeast, and started firing at 1,000 yards [914m] to silence a 20mm gun and crew in front of the hangar. Only a three-second burst was necessary and the gun with two Jerries were out of action for good. I then put the pip on the Me 163 and held the trigger for five seconds, firing up to zero range. The enemy aircraft exploded at the first impact and was burning furiously before I pulled off."

On March 14, 1945, one of the four jet kills was claimed by Captain Donald S. Bryan of the 328th Fighter Squadron, 352nd Fighter Group, who downed one of Germany's new Arado Ar 234 jet bombers. As the Mustangs approached Remagen, Bryan saw the jet as it was approaching the bridgehead. He dropped his tanks and began to follow the jet but could not close the gap. The jet was at least 50mph (80kmph) faster than his Mustang. After watching the German make an abortive low-level bomb run on the bridge, Bryan noticed several P-47s northwest of the Rhine and figured the northbound Ar 234 pilot would see them too and turn eastward to avoid them. Bryan turned his Mustang in a north-easterly direction and waited to spring his trap. The German, almost as if by command, peeled off in an easterly direction. Bryan recounted: "When he passed under me I dove down on him and opened fire at about 250 yards [229m]. I hit him with the first burst and knocked his right jet out. He then made a shallow turn to the right and started a very mild form of evasive maneuvers consisting of shallow turns and a few shallow dives and climbs.

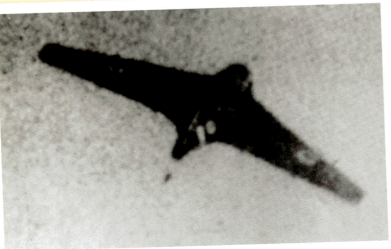

Left: *The revolutionary Messerschmitt Me 163 Komet designed by Alexander Lippisch was the only rocket-powered fighter aircraft ever to have been operational. It was capable of 698mph (1,123kmph).*

Below: *The Messerschmitt Me 262 Schwalbe ("Swallow") was the world's first operational jet-powered fighter aircraft. It was used in a variety of roles, including light bomber, reconnaissance, and even experimental night-fighter versions.*

Above: A self-sealing fuel tank used in the Messerschmitt Me 262A. A British invention, self-sealing tanks automatically plugged tanks holed in combat.

In the afternoon of April 16, 1945, on a heavy bomber mission to Rosenheim, south of Munich, Major Louis H. Norley of the 4th Fighter Group was leading "Cobweb" Squadron (334th): "We gave our box of bombers close escort from rendezvous through the target and back to Ulm and safe airspace, where we broke off escort and set course back to the target area. We cased a previously-planned area, which was an autobahn running south-southeast from Munich. In a section of the wooded area adjacent to the autobahn we found approximately seven fires burning, and eight to ten aircraft parked on the north edge of the woods still intact.

"We reduced altitude from six to 4,000ft [1,219m] and checked them; however the light flak was too accurate and intense to warrant an attack, so we drove on north to Munich to look over Gablingen airfield seen previously. The aircraft parked on this field numbered approximately fifteen; Dornier 217s, a couple of Me 262s, plus a single RAF Halifax bomber, which must have force-landed there. The flak was too vicious to warrant an attack. While we were orbiting, a Me 262 passed 2,000ft [610m] above us heading southeast. I despatched one flight from our group to attempt an engagement, the jet seemingly attempting to land at the aerodrome we were orbiting. The jet managed to escape destruction."

"I fired almost all of my ammo at him and before I had finished I had knocked out his left jet and the jet was emitting much white smoke. I do not believe the aircraft caught fire. At about the time I finished firing the Ar 234 rolled over on its back and dived straight into the ground and exploded. Just before hitting the ground the pilot jettisoned his canopy, but did not get out."

March 21 turned out to be a jet-feast for the 78th Fighter Group, which claimed five Me 262s destroyed, one falling to 1st Lieutenant John A. Kirk III: "Having great faith in the strength of the Mustang, I pulled up the nose so that the gunsight was about one radius above the 262. One quick burst and a check on the wings showed them to be all right, so another fast burst was fired. My bullets must have hit his right engine, as smoke appeared. He slowed up and I anticipated his next move. I then pulled up from my steep dive, hoping to gain on him when he leveled out. He pulled up from his dive and we closed fast. Soon I was in perfect firing range. The guns were fired in long bursts as soon as he was centered in my gunsight. Strikes appeared all along his fuselage and wing roots. Suddenly the pilot seemed to 'pop out' of the cockpit and flew back very close to me. I could see him very well. To record the kill, I took a camera shot of the plane crashing in a ball of flame and the German pilot floating down on his parachute."

Above: Funkgerät FuG 17 radio used in the Messerschmitt Me 262 jet fighter; the radio is on display in the Armádni Muzeum Žižkov in Prague, Czechoslovakia.

"Whispering John" Landers

"When we arrived at least 80 planes were scattered around the field.
When we left there were 80 funeral pyres... German aircraft were blowing up
and burning all over the place. We made eight to nine passes. I scored doubles
on each of my first three passes, two of the six planes blowing up."

—Lieutenant Colonel John D. Landers, April 16, 1945, when fighters of the 8th Air Force
destroyed 752 aircraft; the 78th Fighter Group got 125 of them

In February 1945, Lieutenant Colonel John D. Landers took command of the 78th Fighter Group. The 23-year old Oklahoman had completed two tours, the first in 1942 in the Pacific, where he had destroyed six Japanese aircraft while flying P-40E fighters in the 49th Pursuit Group. After returning to the United States, "Whispering John"— as he was known—was promoted to major and he served as a flight instructor before joining the 38th Squadron, 55th Fighter Group, in late April 1944. Flying P-38J Lightnings he destroyed four German aircraft and damaged another before the group converted to the P-51 Mustang. On October 11, 1944, he transferred to the 357th Fighter Group as group executive and on November 18 he scored his 11th confirmed victory. Landers completed his second tour on December 2 and he returned to the United States, before returning to the ETO to take command of the Duxford outfit on February 22. On March 2, 1945, Landers, flying *Big Beautiful Doll*, scored his first victories with the 78th Fighter Group when he downed two Bf 109s of JG 301 at Burg before gun stoppages prevented further action. "All were freaks" said Landers. "The Jerry pilots were very inexperienced and still played follow the leader."

March 19, 1945, was one of the few occasions that year when Luftwaffe fighters appeared in some strength, when 1,223 American heavies attacked targets in Germany. Landers' forty-eight Mustangs were tasked with freelance bomber support. In the vicinity of Hesepe, three Me 262s attempted to bounce a Mustang squadron in a deliberate attempt to make them to drop their underwing fuel tanks. The Mustangs, however, immediately turned into their attackers without dropping their tanks and the jets soon flew off. A fierce battle raged and the Duxford outfit claimed one of the highest single mission scores in 8th Air Force history, with no fewer than thirty-two enemy aircraft destroyed, two probably destroyed, and sixteen damaged for the loss of two pilots killed. Landers claimed a Bf 109 destroyed for his third group victory and his fourteenth overall.

Left: *Colonel John Landers, the 78th Fighter Group CO from February 22, 1945 to July 1, 1945.*

Below: *Colonel John Landers in the cockpit of "Big Beautiful Doll" attended by two of his faithful ground crew. Born in 1920, Landers attended the Ryan School of Aeronautics in San Diego, California, and actually received his flight wings within days of the Japanese attack on Pearl Harbor.*

On March 30, near Rendsburg airfield Landers spotted an Me 262 1,000ft [304m] on the deck heading south behind him. The CO and his wingman, Lieutenant Thomas V. Thain, dived from 7000ft [2,134m] and bounced the Me 262, which possibly belonged to JG 7. The German pilot made some suicidal gradual turns, which made things easier for Landers and Thain, who queued up and fired into his cockpit almost at will. The German pilot tried to drop his landing gear and he put down on Hohn

Above: A P-51D Mustang—owned and flown by Rob Davies and representing "Big Beautiful Doll" at Duxford flown by John Landers, 78th FG CO—in the sky near Old Buckenham, a wartime B-24 airfield in Norfolk.

Left: Crash-landing by P-51D "Danny Boy" 2 LH-X in the 350th Fighter Squadron, 353rd Fighter Group at Raydon.

airfield, but he crashed and burned without getting out. Landers and Thain shared in the victory, which took the CO's final tally to fourteen and a half victories. On April 10, Colonel Landers led an escort mission in support of B-17 raids on jet fields in the Brandenburg area. After the B-17s had unloaded their bombs on Briest airfield, Landers gave the order to strafe jet airfields in the vicinity and the 78th put in claims for fifty-two enemy aircraft destroyed on the ground. The 82nd Squadron claimed thirty-three of these. Another forty-three enemy aircraft were damaged. Colonel Landers was credited with the destruction of eight aircraft on the ground.

"Storm Bird" Swan Song

On April 16, 1945, fifteen fighter groups provided close and area support for the bombers over Germany and Czechoslovakia. The 78th Fighter Group successfully attacked five enemy airfields in Germany and in the Prague–Pilzen area, and wrought havoc, some of the pilots making up to a dozen strafing runs on the airfields. They claimed no fewer than 135 enemy aircraft destroyed on the ground and a further eighty-nine damaged, and were later awarded a second DUC for the long mission. In all the 8th Air Force fighter groups claimed a record 747 enemy aircraft destroyed for the loss of thirty-four fighters.

Oberleutnant Hans Zepuntke, fighter/fighter-bomber pilot, *Sturmgruppe* JG 4 recalls: "We lined up quickly and did a formation takeoff. Under the prevailing conditions at the airfield this was not always easy, but with 100 percent concentration and mutual trust we had often managed it. We formed up immediately after take-off and departed on a course, climbing up to 3,500m [3,828 yards]. The sunlight was intense and it was unusually hot in the cockpit. After 20 minutes our top cover, flying about 300m [328 yards] above us, reported Mustangs behind us. Everyone looked behind but we were unable to see anything yet. But as I looked to

Left: A Messerschmitt Bf 109 seen through the K-14A gunsight of a Mustang. Through constant development, the Bf 109 remained a formidable foe for Allied fighters throughout the war.

my left, I noticed a Mustang flying straight towards Rudi Rank, as usual at No. 2, diving and firing with all his guns. I snatched my machine around and fired at the enemy aircraft, which broke off at once. But my comrade's machine was on fire and he was already hanging on his parachute.

"Now followed a violent dogfight, during which I succeeded in bringing the Mustang down. Having observed him going down trailing intense smoke, I pulled up steeply to the left. And now my own fate caught up with me. A bullet went through the side window, through my foot, and ended up in the fuel tank. After the first shock I noticed fire on the right side. The cockpit quickly filled with smoke and I could get no air. At this moment I thought that all was finished. But then I jettisoned the cockpit roof, undid my straps, kicked with my left foot against the stick, and jumped out. By then I had suffered second and third degree burns in the face and hands. I pulled the rip-cord of my parachute right away which opened at once. I was hanging there at 3,000m [3,281 yards], below me a huge forested area and not far from that a large lake, about 30km [19 miles] southeast of Konigswuster-hausen [sic]. The aircraft which had shot me down circled a couple of times and then disappeared."

On April 17, thirteen enemy aircraft including four jets were claimed destroyed. In the Prague area 1st Lieutenant Anthony A. Palopoli destroyed an Me 262 on the ground

Left: An Fw 190 fighter lies broken in half on a deserted Luftwaffe airfield in Germany at the end of the war. Poor pilot training in the last months of the war often reduced the effectiveness of this fighter.

Above: *One of the Schwarzemenn or "Black Men," as the German ground crewmen were called because of their black coveralls, rearming a Luftwaffe fighter.*

Right: *The 357th FG CO, Lieutenant Colonel Irwin H. Dregne adds up the score at Leiston for January 14, 1945, when 161 enemy fighters were shot down.*

In total, the American fighters claimed over 250 aircraft destroyed on the ground. It was the last time that the fighter pilots were able to strafe enemy targets because, on the 20th, an order banning attacks of this kind was issued.

Leutnant Fritz R. G. Müller, Me 262 day fighter pilot, credited with six victories in III./JG7 and the Erprobungs Kommando 262, remembers: "We were guided by our own ground control station called 'Sturmvogel', or 'Storm Bird', up to visual contact. If one got into attacking position from behind without being spotted, an *Abschuss* [kill] was assured. But Mustangs and reconnaissance aircraft are no 'barn doors' [four-engined Allied bombers] and the time available for firing was short. Also, one had to pull up sooner than with piston-engined machines, otherwise the victim would disappear up the air intake.

"So, at the beginning, frequently we missed. And if the approach was spotted soon enough by the enemy, their agile aircraft were able to twist or dive away, forcing the jet fighter with its wide turning radius to save his ammunition for another day. To score a hit in such an alerted formation was all but impossible. If the enemy fighter was particularly clever and twisted tightly, he could even throw something at the Messerschmitt. They had noted our weaknesses, but not yet our strengths. That came later. Too late!"

at Cakowice airfield. All told the group destroyed fifteen aircraft on the ground and damaged thirteen more. Two Me 262s were bounced by the flight led by Major Richard "Dick" Hewitt, who chased the 262s for some distance before the jets ran low on fuel and they headed for Kralupy airfield. As the last jet was on its final landing approach Hewitt swept in and shot it down into trees off the end of the single runway. The first Me 262 was still rolling on the far end of the runway as Hewitt set it on fire with a burst of gunfire. By now flak was coming up furiously and his wingman, Allen Rosenblum, was hit as he crossed the airfield. Hewitt recalled: "He crashed, skidding through a hedgerow, shedding the '51's wings and debris flew so bad I figured he had 'had it'. I reported him as a probable KIA at our mission debriefing. Turned out he survived the crash and was taken prisoner. Later he was picked up by an advance Allied tank column as the prisoners were being marched to a PoW camp. Since my gun camera film failed, as it did quite often, I never got kill credit. No eyewitnesses. My jet kills were never officially confirmed. So be it."

The last major air battles between fighter groups of the 8th Air Force and the Luftwaffe took place on April 18, 1945, when 1,211 heavies escorted by more than 1,200 fighters were sent to attack Berlin. Forty Me 262s from JG 7 "Hindenburg" shot down twenty-five bombers with rockets. It was the final challenge by a dying enemy. The Luftwaffe was finished, destroyed in the air and starved of fuel on the ground.

PART 3

R and R

Rest and Recreation

"On a 'forty-eight' [48-hour pass] in London, I left a party at around 11.30 pm to go back to my hotel. Found there was a real bad fog, couldn't see your hand in front of your face in the blackout. Asked a taxi driver to take me back to my hotel but he said with the dimmed lights he had he couldn't see which way to go. So I volunteered to lead the way until he could. Started off walking with one foot on the kerb and the other in the gutter. Ended up walking the whole two miles back to my hotel with this taxi following. When we got there the driver wants full fare and I never even got into his cab!"

—Calvin Hill of the 364th Fighter Group

In Italy the Army Air Corps provided a respite for air crewmen to get away from action at the front. After a defined number of missions, white pilots took leave at a rest camp on the Isle of Capri. The black pilots used a villa in Naples. During leave airmen opted for six days in Naples or three days in Rome. They took sightseeing excursions to Mount Vesuvius and Pompeii. Along with entertainment, USO shows offered another temporary escape, the opportunity to relax, reminisce of home, and enjoy an oasis of Americana in the distant land.

Ramatelli boasted many amenities. There were clubs for both the officers and enlisted men. There were drinks, music, and time to swim in the warm waters of the nearby Adriatic. The home of the 332nd also became the destination for black entertainers and celebrities. Heavyweight boxing champion Joe Louis, himself a sergeant in the US Army, made a courtesy call at the all-black air base. There were movies and USO shows to round out the social life at Ramatelli. At the height of the war, life in the 332nd allowed for pleasant pursuits such as lavish Thanksgiving and Christmas

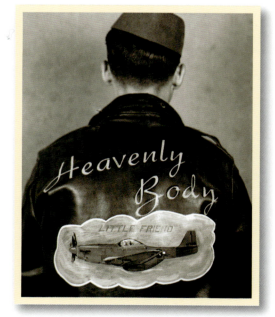

Left: A 401st Bomb Group B-17 crewmember proudly shows off his A-2 jacket "Heavenly Body"; his tribute to the "Little Friends." Originally, the A-2 was to be made of seal-brown horsehide.

dinners, gift packages from home, furloughs to Naples and other Italian cities, and sports competition in the 15th Air Force. Morale remained high, a contrast to the early years in North Africa.

Life in England had become almost as familiar as it had been at home. Brussels sprouts and tea, spam and powered eggs, fish and chips and rare fresh eggs secured from unquestioned sources were part of it, as were intensive poker-playing and crap-shooting early every month, the NAAFI (later replaced by the Red Cross), the Church Army, Betty's and Bunty's. Cambridge had soon acquired the nickname "The 49th State," and the surrounding area was well endowed with historic old inns. GIs liked the public houses and bicycle "sweeps" were frequent to The Plough and John Barleycorn pubs in Duxford village, The Brewery and the Waggon and Horses pubs at Whittlesford Station, and the Flower Pot in Little Abington.

There were dances in Hinxton and Sawston, Whittlesford and Harston, Shelford and Thriplow, Fowlmere and Great Chesterford, Foxton and Melbourn, Abington and Ickleton. Peacetime beer was strong and cheap and most preferred it to spirits or hard liqor as the GIs knew it. Cocktails were almost unknown and iced drinks were regarded with horror. All pubs closed by law at 22:30 hours.

would come out and close the gates several minutes before the train was scheduled. After the train passed, but not real soon after, the old men would come slowly out and open the gates.

"That's where we caught the train to London, which we did pretty frequently. There were houses run by the Red Cross or somebody where we could always get a room. We could eat at the Grosvenor House Hotel. The ballroom was converted to a huge cafeteria, which always fed hundreds of American officers. There were plenty of places to see, Westminster Abbey, St Paul's, Madame Tussaud's and countless other places. My favorite theater was the 'Windmill', guess why! London was blacked out so the light was dim with practically no traffic or noise. Once I climbed up to the whispering gallery in St Paul's and while the attendant was whispering, a V-2 hit close outside. The attendant said, 'That was close, wasn't it?' It was…"

Left: US airmen enjoy a quiet moment rowing their way through Cambridge, a popular haunt for Americans on R&R.

Below and top: The Quintone 'Spit n' Polish' cleaning kit was most useful, but GIs were known to clean their ODs (wool uniforms) in aviation gas. On the days pilots did not fly, aviators had either powdered eggs or "S-O-S" with biscuits and powdered milk.

"The Eagle" in Benet Street in Cambridge beckoned, with its smoked ceiling revealing RAF and USAAF squadron numbers and nicknames. Drummer Street and the Bull Hotel, the Rex Ballroom and the Dorothy, the Cam and Cambridge parks, the smell of mild and bitter and the odor from the fishmongers.

"Life at Duxford wasn't all flying by any means," recalled Captain Pete Keillor. "We all had bicycles and there were plenty of roads to ride on. You could head out in any direction and find a village within 5 miles [8km] and then you could turn, go to another village and come back on a different road.

"Duxford was the name of the airfield and also the nearby village. There was an old church that was only used occasionally. It had been replaced by the new church, which was three hundred years old. The closest town was Whittlesford, which we referred to as the bottleneck of the ETO. Trains came through frequently and two old men

"The war wasn't all work and no play," remembered Larry Nelson. "Many celebrities visited our base under the direction of the United Service Organization (USO). These included the famous Bob Hope, Frances Langford, Bing Crosby, and Marlene Dietrich, who came at various times to Duxford. This was a huge occasion for all of us.

"From time-to-time we would go into town. Our two social cities were Cambridge and London. In London I was not successful getting a BELT [bacon, fried egg, lettuce, and tomato sandwich] but I did find a girl. Her name was Pat Messenger. Little did I know at the time that she was dating an RCAF flyer on alternate weekends from me. Later I learned from her mother how careful Pat was to keep our identities separate from each other and she married her RCAF flyer.

"Cambridge is known for its colleges and for punting on the Cam but what most of us GIs remember was the very popular Dorothy Dance Hall. There were plenty of girls to dance with at the Dorothy. The place was

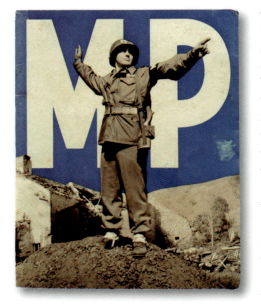

always jumping, especially on a Saturday night. I guess the English girls needed to have a little fun and they sure did love to dance. We had a number of weddings as the result of these get-togethers at the Dorothy. Before going to the dance hall, I usually met up with Don Freer, a hometown friend who flew B-17s from Bassingbourn nearby. We met to talk about what was happening back home and our week of flying missions, many of which we flew together. Then one day in December, Don didn't come back from his mission. I found out later that he had been shot down and taken prisoner. It was great that he survived. Too many of my friends did not make it back from their missions."

On February 1, 1944, Frank O'Connor and Richard E. Turner in the 354th Fighter Group at Boxted got a three-day pass to explore London. "We dressed in our most presentable Class A uniforms," recalled Turner, "wheedled a few loans from among our less fortunate comrades, arranged transportation into Colchester from the squadron transportation officer; and caught the train for London.

"Arriving at Victoria Station we hailed a cab and proceeded to what one of our friends had called a private hotel, recommending it highly. Upon registering we were politely informed that for £5 apiece we would have the second floor suite with breakfast for ourselves and guests. Up in

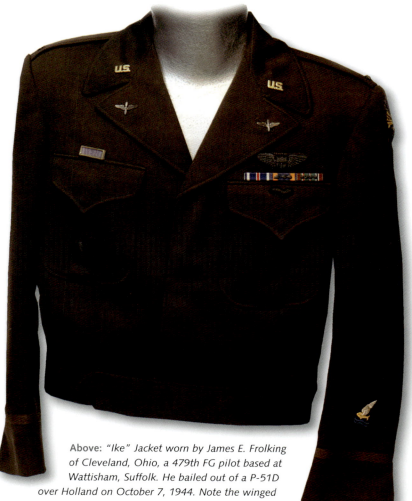

Above: *"Ike" Jacket worn by James E. Frolking of Cleveland, Ohio, a 479th FG pilot based at Wattisham, Suffolk. He bailed out of a P-51D over Holland on October 7, 1944. Note the winged goldfish on the sleeve. Frolking finally made it back to his home base on November 4, 1944. The Ike jacket was named after General Dwight D. Eisenhower, who asked that an improved version with concealed buttons and sharper appearance be developed for the ETO and MTO as both a service and field jacket.*

Left: *A booklet explaining the roles and duties of the Military Policeman, an individual who kept a close eye on off-duty US personnel.*

the suite Frank wondered what they had meant by guests? I told him that the word meant the same thing here as it did in the US and Frank pointed out the fact that we didn't know anyone in London to invite as guests for breakfast. I ventured that the English evidently had ample confidence in the gregarious nature of American pilots since there had evidently been a few here before us. At any rate, freshly scrubbed and armed with hope, Frank and I set out for the pubs. We investigated every female available in every spot we hit, with a date for the evening's festivities in mind, but our every tactic was expertly countered.

"We ended up the evening congregating with other luckless pilots, trying hard to drink the pubs dry and telling one another how our unit was ridding the skies of the Luftwaffe. The stories were usually interrupted at least once a night while we dove under the nearest table to wait out an air-raid—a peculiarly frequent performance for a Luftwaffe that had been chased from the skies so often. Little inconsistencies like this didn't bother us a bit and the stories became more exaggerated as the night went on. As a rule we ended up in our suite like the good boys our mothers firmly believed us to be, sleeping through those wonderful breakfasts that had been so generously offered with our lodgings. In fact, on the train back to base Frank made the astute observation that 'If this war lasts long enough those people are going to become millionaires on unserved breakfasts!'"

Following the mission of April 5, 1944, the 336th Squadron's medical officer suggested that Johnny Godfrey take seven days' leave to rest and relax after his lengthy stretch of combat flying. Johnny recalled: "He had been watching me for some time. The twitching about my eyes and mouth was now quite noticeable and my hands trembled. It was nothing serious if caught in time. A week's rest away from the base, away from its tense excitement, was what the doctor recommended. If I would like to spend my time in a 'flak' home, arrangements would be made. That wasn't for me; most of the boys there were from bomber crews, who suffered more from the shakes than fighter pilots.

"I packed my bag and caught the 5.15pm train from Audley End for London, checked in at the Prince's Garden Club and then set out for some R and R in London. Have you ever spent some time at a place where every minute was filled with joy, where even the air seemed different and exciting—then return later to the same place to find that everything has changed? Actually, it hadn't changed—it was probably the same but your perspective had altered so that now everything seemed drab and dull. That was my reaction. The same bars were jammed with

people, but the faces were those of strangers. The war had taken its toll and the boys whom I had trained and flown with were few and far between. The girls seemed old, and the few I did meet who I recognized had no appeal for me now. Even the drinks didn't taste the same, and regardless of how many I downed I couldn't recapture what it was I was looking for. Disgustedly, I walked alone through the dark streets from Piccadilly to the Prince's Garden Club."

England in Focus

Here is a civilian version of the Kodak 35 Anastar Special Camera in standard production finish, procured for the USAAF in 1943. It was a popular wartime model used by the Signal Corps. The majority of army cameramen used the Speed Graphic camera and not until late in the war did the use of 35mm photographic equipment become popular. Photography was a relatively cheap occupation. On return from a 48-hour pass or leave GIs could get their films of London, Cambridge, and other Liberty towns developed for free or favor in the base photo lab.

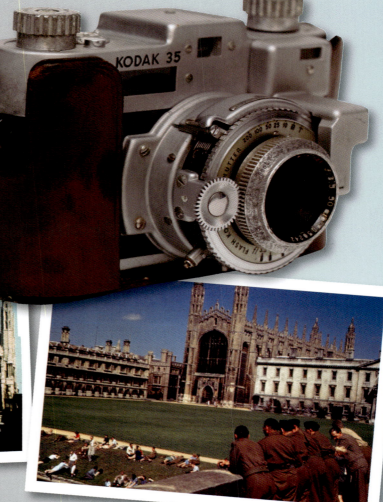

Above left: The American Red Cross Club (Bull Hotel) in Trumpington Street, Cambridge. The city boasted six clubs, five for enlisted men and one for officers. **Above right:** *GIs on a bridge over the Cam at Kings College in Cambridge, where the Provost often recounted the history of the college to invited American guests from bases in East Anglia.*

Duxford Social Life

"The ground crews lived together so long, we became family, sharing everything, the good, bad and in between. Working long hard hours, we still had lots of fun together. Each cot was put in the same general area in the barracks. The barracks walls were well decorated with pin-up girls such as Betty Grable, Rita Hayworth, Lana Turner, Alexis Smith, and Vargas calendar girls. Popular dance bands heard on Armed Forces Radio helped relaxing after the day."

—James Tudor, crew chief, 78th Fighter Group at Duxford

As usual after a big day, nearly everyone on the base who was feeling pretty good made for the clubs and bars on base. Officers retired to the Officers' Club, the sergeants to the Sergeants' Club, others to the Aeroclub or Duffy's Tavern, the mixing pot of the base. Over glasses of beer (specially brewed for Duxford) many a mission was retold, many a ball game was replayed, many a T.S. [Tough Shit] problem was aired, commented on, and the accompanying "T.S. slip" dutifully punched. Captain W. L. "Duffy" Owen, who doubled as station athletic officer, was a frequent host and bull-shooter.

The Officers' Club housed mess and kitchens, a comfortable lounge, card rooms, recreational rooms, and a bar. The dining room had become a dance floor for parties. When the sun did shine the front terrace and lawns were popular for lounging and sun bathing. The Aeroclub was everybody's meeting place. Coffee hour in the morning found everyone gathered together over rolls and coffee, swapping rumors, trading news and gripes. Downstairs was a large snack bar and lounge (used for dances three nights each month), kitchens and staff quarters, and a small lounge named the "State Room," used by officers during the day and for small social functions each evening. A stage opened into the snack bar and the second floor was devoted to a library, reading and writing rooms, lounge, barber shop, and offices.

The Sergeants' Club had a modern, half-circular bar, lounge, card room, and billiard room. A ballroom was used for the monthly dances, for ping-pong games, as additional lounge space, and for private parties. On cool nights, groups of men gathered around the several fireplaces in the club to sip beer and swap tales and experiences.

Left: To GIs, British beer tasted like it was watered down; there was no head! The higher the alcohol content the less carbonation, ergo the flat taste. Mild beer was weak, watery, and warm.

Right: Hand held Revere Standard 8mm Ciné Camera manufactured by the Revere Camera Company of Chicago; such cameras were used by GIs on leave and when on base.

There was a light drizzle when Bing Crosby's USO troupe performed a show at one of the single-bay Belfast hangar entrances that had been converted into a theater by the RAF and used for dances and shows. Many traveling shows requested Duxford as one of their stops because of the theater's fine dressing rooms and stage, and large seating capacity. Apart from Bing Crosby the theater was to host several well-known stars of the cinema and radio such as James Cagney, Bob Hope, and Tommy Farr. Refinements like this made Duxford one of the most comfortable AAF bases overseas and helped foster a "Country Club" atmosphere.

"Free time for the troops was available once your plane was secured for the day," recalls James Tudor. "We had permanent passes to use when we were off. They just required you to sign out in the orderly room before leaving. A big 6 x 6 GI truck left the base at 6:00pm for Cambridge and picked up between 11:00 and 12:00pm for return to the base. Favorite GI haunts on base were The Sergeant Club, Duffy's Tavern, NAAFI-Red Cross Aero Club, Church Army, and Betty and Bunty's Cafe. Establishments the GIs were fond of in Cambridge proper included the Red Lion pub on Trumpington Road, Bull Hotel (Red Cross Club), Dorothy's Cafe, American Bar, the Criterion, and the Rex Ballroom. There we congregated with many of the bomber crews and hashed out the

Above right: *A deathly pall of smoke marks the end of a B-17 flown by a bomber pilot with two fighter pilots from Duxford on board after control was lost during a "beat up."*

Right: *American Red Cross clubs were hotels for the US military. They were clean and completely adequate, plus they served free coffee and donuts all day and night.*

missions of the day, drank Mild & Bitter, threw darts and sang. The bars closed at 10:00 pm and after singing 'God Save the King', many of us queued up for fish and chips wrapped in newspapers..."

"The first thing the Debden soldier did," recalled Grover C. Hall Jr, "was to make for the local at the Rose and Crown to order a scotch and soda. 'Sorry,' the barmaid would answer, 'you've had it.' He would reply: 'Had it, did you say? I just got here.' Somebody would then explain that 'had it' is RAF'ese for you're out of luck, or it's all gone there ain't no more.

"At Audley End Station he bought a ticket for Liverpool Street Station for his first 48-hour pass to London and squeezed on the 5:15. There was

standing room only on the trains, a condition that would have prevailed even if the Britons had put their newspapers down. At first the soldier didn't know West End from The City, so he queued up for one of those faded blue cabs that sit up high and gadabout like a maiden aunt come vis-a-vis with a long-lost lover. Later, when it was ruefully discovered that a British pound sterling is not equivalent to a dollar bill green, he

learned to ride the Underground, savoring the names of the stops as he went … Ealing Broadway … Knightsbridge … Marble Arch … Chancery Lane … Elephant and Castle … Charing Cross … Oxford Circus … Piccadilly Circus … East Acton … Bank.

"On the first trip he started out to do all the historic spots, like the haunts of Dr Johnson, Goldsmith, and Rare Ben Jonson. He viewed the Blitz scars but was forbidden by the censors to write home about them. He sauntered through the ineffable Piccadilly Circus,

Top: Despite suffering under years of austerity, London still provided a world of attractions to off-duty airmen. Above: Strand Underground (Tube) station. Left: Personnel at East Wretham in Norfolk take a "48 [hour] To London" on the steam train service.

capital of America-in-Britain, Leicester Square, the Strand, and tiptoed through Westminster Abbey. He took a gander at the Mother of Parliaments and set his watch by Big Ben. He progressed along Birdcage Walk to Buckingham Palace to see the changing of the guards. He whistled up a taxi, the approved method being a trumpeted 'tax-HEE'.

'Take me to 221-B Baker Street.'

"This archness is old stuff to the driver, but he drives there anyway. The fare found neither Dr Watson nor Holmes at home, which is probably elementary anyway. Probably out getting the usual 7 percent cocaine pick-me-up.

"If he were an officer, he had more or less had it insofar as sightseeing went. On subsequent '48s' he headed straight for the Jules Club on Jermyn Street, or to any of a most formidable array of places he was able to establish himself in. It's just possible that he proceeded to a lecture on the early history of the Belgian Parliament but if a quorum were needed, it was best to start searching at the Cracker's Club—that dingy little Piccadilly hole with the smell of a 'Y' gym through which half the Allies' fighter pilots passed and wrote their names on the walls—and wind through the Studio Club, Lansdowne House, the Garter, Wellington, Embassy, and Astor Clubs.

"Ah, but the enlisted man on furlough—he covered England like the dew covers Dixie. He was an authentic grassroots plenipotentiary. He was everywhere and stood short nowhere. With less money to spend but with just as much time off as officers, the enlisted soldier saw twice as much of the country and knew its people that much better.

"In Piccadilly Circus, about Rainbow Corner, you couldn't see even the big 'Bovril' sign for the American olive drab. They walked about with the girls of many nationalities on their arms. White-helmeted MPs—a source of ceaseless delight and fascination to Englishmen—stood in the entrances to the Underground, which blew its dank breath into the street and lay in wait for GIs with unbuttoned blouses or one more mild and bitter than they could carry. Through the incredibly congested Circus the lavender-and-old lace cabs would rage, packed with Americans. You could tell the new arrivals because they rode in clusters of five to eight with the top down, waving a bottle of Scotch and causing the Limeys to remark, 'See? The Americans are the reason spirits are in short supply.'

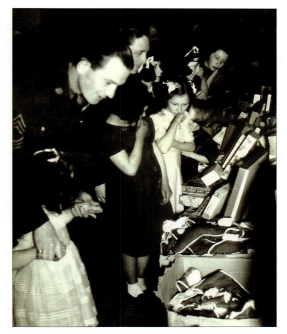

Above left: A black GI dancing with an English girl caused trouble among the white GIs and only segregated "liberty towns" for the races ceased tensions. Above right: A kids' Christmas party at the 355th Fighter Group's base at Steeple Morden.

Left: Third Liberty Loan badge. Slogans like "Back the Attack!" urged US citizens to buy US Defense bonds every payday. In May 1942 sales exceeded that month's goal of $600 million. By the time the Fifth War Loan was launched on D-Day, June 6, 1944, the ante had been raised to $16 million in bonds.

Left: Conductor's Bell on a London bus. Red London buses and their drivers and "clippies" (conductresses) were popular with GIs on leave in the capital. All too soon the two-day vacation from the war would come to an end and they would return to combat somewhat hung over.

"Night would fall and Piccadilly would assume the shape, which will always be a flashing memory with those who did time in the ETO. The blackout was rigid, or at least it would have been had it not been for thousands of GIs hurrying about with their torches (Limey for flashlight). You could tell an American from any other in the dark because their flashlights were larger and more powerful. From Lower Regent Street, they made Piccadilly look like a jar of fireflies in a closet. The Leicester Square theater queues would grow even longer, reaching down Shaftesbury Avenue almost to Piccadilly.

"At first blackout the celebrated 'Piccadilly Commandos' would begin walking the night, as much a part of the scene as the doorman in front of the Regent Palace Hotel. Inappropriately, the famous statue of Eros, God of Love, was crated during the war. They were more an institution than a facility and few GIs (I speak for Debden) permitted themselves a conclusive encounter. They were as alert as a bell captain and aggressive, approaching everything in olive drab with a parroted American slang greeting which was ridiculous when conveyed on a British accent. Their honorariums were enormous (and downright incredible when they walked under a light). But they were an integral part of Piccadilly's teeming, fetid pageantry. A Debden corporal wrote a song, 'Lilly from Piccadilly', which the ETO sang.

"Soon the soldier began to feel at home, the first sign being that he spent two days in London without gawking at the barrage balloons loafing over the city. He got caught in air raids and learned to tell the big ones from the little ones by the whistle. He became allergic to exposed lights and blacked them out with reflex action. He began counting British currency as easily as US. There was just one thing whose hatefulness never diminished, the weather. Every day he felt as though his skin had accumulated another layer of mold.

"Isn't there some Kipling about 'single men in barracks don't grow into plaster saints?' Anyway, there were 1,500 officers and men at Debden, for the most part high-spirited American males between the ages of 20 and 30, some 3,000 miles removed from home and trying to forget the fact. Some arrived as virtuosos of the secular life, while others maintained the pretense until they got the hang of it."

As a country boy who spent his youth in Burlington, a small town in North Carolina, all of Clarence "Buck" G. Haynes' time in England "was one of enlightenment and pleasure. I joined the Air Corps on September 23, 1942, and received my wings on February 8, 1944. After being trained as a fighter pilot, I arrived at Prestwick about August 3, 1944 and then went to Stone for a few days processing. Then it was to Goxhill near Hull for check-out in a Mustang. I went to Wattisham about September 1 and was assigned to 434th Fighter Squadron, 479th Fighter Group. It was a hell of an exciting time and learning just how war takes place was an eye-opener. My first mission was Berlin on September 28.

"I appreciated being lucky enough to live in permanent quarters with steam heat, 60ft [18m] to the mess and a beautiful lounge. There were Liberty Runs to Ipswich in the black out—hair-raising!—to attend movies. The first and subsequent trips to London were out of this world for a little ol' country boy. I had always been a people-watcher so you could imagine me in London. My first trip to London was with three others and only one had been there before.

"We arrived there in the dark at Liverpool Street station and took our first taxi to the West End, having our wits scared out of us as we dodged other blacked out taxis and buses. We were naïve enough to think that we might just get a room at the Savoy. After all, we were now one of those 'over-paid', 'over fed', 'over-sexed,' and 'over there' Yanks. We soon realized that we were slightly out of our class so we headed for the American Red Cross Jules Officers Club in Jermyn Street near Piccadilly Circus. Nice polite English ladies welcomed us and soon we had consumed hot tea and coffee and donuts. Then off to a narrow cot with 'biscuits' and clean sheets.

"At the time London was the center of the universe. Our first sightseeing was the Palace, Westminster and the Parliament buildings. Our first dinner was at the Grosvenor House where food was delicious and cheap. Our first show was at the Palladium. At Peale's Bootery one of our group, Harold Jenkins, paid $50 for a hand-made knee-high pair of boots. I couldn't even entertain the thought of paying one week's pay for something to go on my feet but they were beautiful.

"About February 1945 I visited Dan, a lieutenant friend of mine who was assigned to 8th Air Force HQ at High Wycombe. His girlfriend had made a picnic lunch and set up another girl and the four of us went on a hike and in a glade near a golf course we spread our 'feast' of bread, butter and jam. On return to Jermyn Street Dan paired me up with Andy, our flight engineering officer. We headed for Liverpool Street station and while waiting for them to open the platform gate I observed three WAAFs who were 'in the same boat' as us.

"We agreed to watch which carriage they entered and then, by 'coincidence', ended up opposite each other in the same

Above: Americans found British telephone boxes bemusing, especially when the operator said "You're through Yank!" which in British English meant "you are connected" but in American it means you're finished!.

Right: Peppermint flavored Beech-Nut gum wrapper given to a Clacton boy. "Got any gum chum" was the popular refrain of British kids who were often asked in return, "Got a sister mister?"

for our trip back to Ipswich. Andy was quite nicely married and me not being a personality kid, we slowly commenced a conversation with three reserved English girls. The train huffed and puffed through the different stops and about the time I learned Margory's name she informed me that Colchester was her station and from there they would have a two-hour walk to their huts. 'Marge' was a telephone operator and she had spent 28 months in Northern Ireland before being re-assigned to Earls Colne in Essex. I think my first attraction to Marge was her smile and general demeanor. And she didn't smoke.

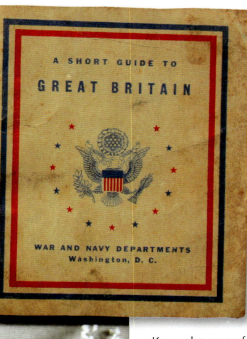

A SHORT GUIDE TO
GREAT BRITAIN

WAR AND NAVY DEPARTMENTS
Washington, D. C.

"We would frequent a small restaurant called 'Athens' where we enjoyed 'good' horse steak—it got better all the time. There was a famous stage comedian called Sid Field, who we saw a couple of times. He had this little country boy in stitches from laughing so much. Having grown up in such austere times and conditions, sometimes I thought I had died and gone to heaven. One of my biggest regrets was not having more knowledge of English history. Learning more and more about English sacrifices was interesting. Marge's dad was a volunteer warden and her brother Ken, who was of my age, had been killed on a bombing raid over Germany in 1942.

"Because of the long days Andy let me take a Mustang down to Marks Hall and spend a short visit. My departures would usually be a little 'Smart Alec' but the tower seemed to enjoy them. I also knew where Marge's hut was so I gave them an occasional 'low pass.'

"When England was planning to celebrate Battle of Britain day on September 15, 1946, a contingent of aircraft from our base was to participate. However, I was only a spare pilot so we decided it would be a pretty good time to tie the knot. We had four days to arrange a marriage. I left for Neubiberg about 10 miles [16km] from Munich but Marge had to go through the usual red tape to procure a military pass et cetera, and so started married life in a country we had just been at war with. It was an experience. However, we both survived!"

Above and top: Meeting the folks. At the war's end hundreds of British war brides left the United Kingdom for a new life with their GI husbands in all parts of America. "A Short Guide To Great Britain" War and Navy Departments, Washington DC, (top) was a booklet issued to every GI arriving in Britain in 1942.

"We had a phone in the hall of our quarters and so our relationship grew. Soon we would meet each other at the bus station in Colchester, have a nice dinner at a quaint hotel on the High Street just above the Roman ruins, maybe see a movie and then back to Ipswich. We didn't date a great deal but when we had time off we would go to London and I would stay at Marge's home in North Finchley. Movies and sightseeing occupied most of our time. We expanded our sightseeing to Hampton Court, via the Thames, Crystal Palace, and many others.

The 359th Fighter Group History described the "48 To London": "Brandon, Lakenheath, Shippea Hill, Ely, Cambridge, Audley End, Bishop's Stortford, LONDON." One airman remembered: "There was the time you stood from Thetford all the way to London, your feet numb in the draughty corridor, the windows steamed so that even the bleak Suffolk landscape was hidden in the November curtain of cold. There was the jerking, stopping, backing, starting and there was the inevitable twenty-minute stop at Ely. You cursed the heat-lever over the seat; it never worked. But then it was April, a half-year later. You left your overcoat behind in the belly-tank crate that served as a wall-locker, stuffed some shaving articles in your musette bag and hopped the 5.50

or the 9 or the 11 o'clock bus from the MP Gate. You were taking off on a '48 to London.' It was spring and you felt eager.

"No tickets now at 14-bob-round-trip. In April '45 you began getting reverse Lend-Lease in travel warrants to any point in the UK. You waited on the platform for the train to pull in from Norwich, buying a 'Daily Express,' 'Sketch,' 'Mail,' 'Post' or 'Illustrated.' Then you read the signs, 'There'll Always Be Mazawattee Tea' and watched a Thetford farmer herd two goats off the Bury train through the passengers. And you looked over the local civilians, the British officers and the scores of American airman, a few of them with all their gear starting the trip back to the States.

"Local trains from Swaffham and Watton arrived with school-kids in shorts and high wool stockings, clutching their books like the school-kids in all countries. The British Indian soldiers looked up from the freight cars they were unloading and silently watched the trains. Thetford is a small town, but its station carried life in and out by day and night: girls from Knettishall, Scotch [sic] officers in kilts, GIs starting on pass clean-shaven and returning un-pressed, unshaven and unwell; goats, dogs, bicycles, and boxes of aromatic fish.

"And there was the morning a few months after D-Day when your train was an hour late and then you saw why: A hospital train steamed in to pick up a score of US wounded, casualties headed for the States. There was no ceremony, no coffee and doughnuts or brave smiles. The wounded stared back at those who stared at them, their eyes dull and tired…

"You sat in the compartment and slept most of the way. That is you sat when there was a seat, one of the eight that could be crowded into each compartment. Opposite you was a minister who smiled in a kindly, professional way; three gunners from the B-17 field near Bury, invariably sleeping; two civilian women next to you reading a cheap-covered book and holding boxes and babies; a civilian smoking steadily, his pipe acrid and penetrating, tobacco shreds sprinkled unnoticed on his well-worn overcoat. Again you read the signs in the train… 'If danger seems imminent, lie on the floor,' advised the poster next to the water-colour of the cathedral. 'It is dangerous for passengers to put their heads out of carriage windows,' warned the message over the door with the window you opened by working the heavy leather strap."

On trips to London, Arthur "Art" Swanson of the 357th Fighter Group got to know the underground system very well. "Sometimes I'd

Above: *Dancing at the Aero Club on base, with girls invited from local towns and villages, was always popular with both sexes.*

Left: *A GI production of the musical "Skirts" which toured many of the towns and cities near American bases in East Anglia in 1944–45.*

see Britishers standing around on a platform looking lost. I'd go up and offer to give directions. Got a kick out of the look on their faces when a Yank told them which train to catch.

"Like most young Americans of my time I went looking for adventure and was certainly not afraid of strange places or customs. Naturally the main focus for adventures was the opposite sex. On my first evening pass after arriving at Raydon I went to Colchester. There I got into conversation with a girl I met in the main street and we got along famously. She was married to a British soldier who was serving overseas but this fact didn't appear to inhibit her.

"On the next date she brought along her sister who appeared most anxious to meet a Yank. Here I was with two girls and one was all I could handle. So I had to do some fast thinking. We were outside the Red Cross Club in Colchester and just then I happened to see a GI come out the door. I told the girls to wait where they were while I walked over to this guy and said, 'Are you interested in a real nice date?' My luck was in: 'Hell, yes!' he said. So I took him over and introduced him to the girls; 'This is a good buddy of mine.' The truth was I'd never before seen him in my life. Could hardly see him anyway because of the blackout—couldn't see the sister for that matter. Anyhow, these two paired up and solved my problem.

"A very nice friendship developed with the Colchester girl but our stay at Raydon was short and the group moved to another base 25 miles [40km] northeast. Around this time I was sent up to a base near Grimsby on detached service. To get there I had to first catch a train to London. Being a city boy I took the opportunity to look around and decided this was the place for me. So from then on whenever I got my monthly three-day pass I was off to London. Found a nice

little pub in Kensington High Street. The blonde at the back of the bar took my fancy and I thought maybe I can do something here. I started by buying her drinks and it was soon obvious the interest was mutual. She was another married girl and her husband was a Jap prisoner, having been picked up at Singapore. We dated regularly and she brightened life considerably for this 22-year-old. Thousands of miles from home and without the inhibiting influence of family and the local community, there was no check on the randy tendencies of a young man at that time of life.

"I could usually only get to London once a month and there were attractions nearer to hand. When Jerry started launching buzz-bombs from out over the North Sea, the British moved in AA guns around our base, which was close to the coast. Several of these batteries were partly crewed by ATS [Auxiliary Territorial Service] girls. For us GIs it was like shooting fish in a barrel, there were so many of these girls at the social events. We also discovered the Palais de Dance at Lowestoft, a small port with a heavy Royal Navy presence. Fourteen of us went there to give a buddy who had volunteered for the infantry a good send-off. Whether it was the glasses of gin and orange or the GIs that attracted them I don't know, but we soon found we had a host of the navy girls, Wrens, round our table. However, my local attraction was an air force girl, a WAAF who was based at the radar directional station near Dunwich. She was single, a nice girl and good fun. Yes, I enjoyed my adventures in England."

Left and top: The headlines say it all. The massive celebrations in Piccadilly Circus on Victory in Europe (VE) Day—May 8, 1945—were, for many people, colored by memories of those who didn't survive the war.

Further Reading

Air Ministry. *The Rise and Fall of the German Air Force 1933–1945* (London, 1948)

Bekker, Cajus. *The Luftwaffe War Diaries* (Da Capo, 1994)

Boiten, Theo and Bowman, Martin W. *Raiders of the Reich. Air Battle Western Europe: 1942–1945* (Airlife, 1996)

Boiten, Theo and Bowman, Martin W. *Battles With the Luftwaffe* (Janes, 2001)

Bowman, Martin W. *Great American Air Battles of WW2* (Airlife, 1994)

Bowman, Martin W. *Four Miles High* (PSL, 1992)

Bucholtz, Chris. *332nd Fighter Group—Tuskegee Airmen* (Osprey, 2007)

Cora, Paul B. *Yellowjackets! The 361st Fighter Group in World War II* (Schiffer, 2002)

Dibbs, John M. and Grey, Stephen. *Flying Legends P-51 Mustang* (MBI, 2002)

Donald, William, and Burn, John. *One-Zero-Five...'* (GMS Enterprises, 2005)

Colgan, William B. *Allied Strafing in WWII: A Cockpit View of Air To Ground Battle* (McFarland & Co. Inc., 2010)

Cross, G. E. *Jonah's Feet Are Dry: The Experiences of the 353rd Fighter Group during WWII* (Thunderbolt Publishing, 2001)

Davis, Larry. *P-51 Mustang In Action.* (Squadron Signal, 1981)

Duxford Diary 1942–45 (W. Heffer & Sons, 1945)

Fairfield, Terry A. *The 479th Fighter Group in WW2 in Action over Europe with the P-38 & P-51* (Schiffer 2004)

Fry, Garry L. and Ethell, Jeffrey L. *Escort To Berlin;The 4th Fighter Group in WWII* (Arco Publishing Inc., 1980)

Goebel, Robert J. *Mustang Ace,* (Zenith, 1991)

Gotts, Steve. *Little Friends: A Pictorial History of the 361st Fighter Group in WW2* (Taylor Publishing, 1993)

Gruenhagen, Robert W. *Mustang: The Story of the P-51 fighter* (Arco, 1976)

Hall, Grover C., *One Thousand Destroyed* (Morgan Aviation Books, 1946)

Hardesty, Von. *Black Wings; Courageous Stories of African Americans in Aviation and Space History* (Smithsonian, 2008)

Hess, Bill, *Aces and Wingmen II* (Aviation Usk, 1999)

Homan, Lynn M. and Reilly, Thomas. *Black Knights: The Story of the Tuskegee Airmen* (Pelican Publishing Co, 2001)

Jarrett, Philip. *Aircraft of the Second World War* (Putnam, 1997)

Kaplan, Philip. *Two-Man Air Force* (Pen & Sword Aviation, 2006)

Long, Eric F. *At The Controls* (Airlife 2001)

McGee-Smith, Charlene E. Ph.D. *Tuskegee Airman: The Biography of Charles E. McGee* (Branden Publishing, 1999)

McKissack, Patricia and Frederick. *Red-Tail Angels: The Story of the Tuskegee Airmen of World War II* (Walker & Company, 1995)

McLachlan, Ian. *USAAF Fighter Stories.* (Haynes Publishing, 1997)

McLachlan, Ian. *USAAF Fighter Stories: A New Selection* (Sutton Publishing, 2005)

Miller, Kent D. *The 363rd Fighter Group in WWII In Action over Europe with the P-51 Mustang* (Schiffer, 2002)

Mombeek, Eric. *Defending The Reich: The History of JG 1 "Oesau"* (JAC Publications 1992)

Morgan, Len. *P-51 Mustang: Famous Aircraft Series* (Morgan Aviation Books, 1963)

Morris, Danny *Aces and Wingmen Volume I* (Aviation SK, 1989)

Nowarra, Heinz J. *The Focke-Wulf 190: A Famous German Fighter* (Harleyford 1965)

Nijboer, Donald. *Cockpit: An Illustrated History* (Airlife, 1998)

O'Leary, Michael. *VIII Fighter Command At War "Long Reach"* (Osprey Publishing, 2000)

Olynyk, Frank. *Stars & Bars: A Tribute to the American Fighter Ace 1920–1973* (Grub Street 1995)

Patterson, Michael. *Battle for the Skies: From Europe to the Pacific* (David & Charles, 2004)

Powell, R. H. *The Blue Nosed Bastards of Bodney* (Privately Published, 1990)

Price, Dr. Alfred. *Luftwaffe Handbook 1939–1945* (Ian Allan, 1986)

Scutts, Jerry. *Mustang Aces of the Eighth Air Force* (Osprey Publishing, 1994)

Shores, Christopher and Williams, Clive. *Aces High: A Tribute to the Most Notable Fighter Pilots of the British and Commonwealth Forces in WWII* (Grub Street, 1994)

Smith, J. R. and Kay, Antony *German Aircraft of the Second World War* (Putnam, 1972)

Smith, Peter C. *Straight Down! The North American A-36 dive-bomber in Action* (Crécy Publishing, 2000)

Speer Frank E. *The Debden Warbirds: The 4th Fighter Group in WWII* (Schiffer 1999)

Spick, Mike. *Luftwaffe Fighter Aces* (Ivy Books, 1996)

Stanaway, John. *479th Fighter Group "Riddles Raiders"* (Osprey Publishing, 2009)

Swanborough, G. & Green, William. *The Focke-Wulf 190* (Arco, 1986)

Wagner, Ray, *American Combat Planes* (Doubleday & Co. 1982)

Wells, Ken, *Steeple Morden Strafers 1943–45* (East Anglian Books, 1994)

Wood, Tony & Gunston, Bill, *Hitler's Luftwaffe* (Random House, 1979)

Glossary

2nd TAF 2nd Tactical Air Force (RAF)

A&AEE Aeroplane & Armament Experimental Establishment (British)

Abschuss Confirmed victory in air combat

AI Airborne Intercept (radar)

Alarmstart Scramble

ALG Advanced Landing Ground

ASR Air-Sea Rescue (British)

BG Bomb Group

bogies enemy aircraft

CAVU Ceiling and Visibility Unlimited

CBI China–Burma–India Theater

CBO Combined Bomber Offensive

Diver V-1 flying bomb

The Drink The sea

E/A Enemy aircraft

Eagle Squadron RAF squadrons composed of American volunteer pilots before the USA entered the war.

Eichenlaub (El) Knight's Cross with Oak Leaves

Eisernes Kreuz 1, II (EK I, EK II) Iron Cross (1st and 2nd Class)

Einsatz Operational flight

Erganzungsgruppe (EGr) Replacement or complement wing

ETO European Theater of Operations

Experte(n) (German) an ace or aces

Express-Express R/T code for "hurry up"

Flak (Flieger Abwehr Kanonen) Anti-aircraft artillery

Führer Leader

Geschwader Roughly equivalent to three RAF wings. Comprises three or four Gruppen

GI General Issue; a US serviceman

Gruppe Group containing three or four Staffeln, designated by Roman figures eg. IV./JG 26

Gruppenkommandeur Commander or captain, a Gruppe command position rather than a rank

HE High-explosive (bomb)

Heavies Bombers

HEI High-explosive incendiary (bomb)

IAS Indicated air speed

IFF Identification friend or foe

IO Intelligence officer

IP Initial point at the start of the bomb run

Jagdgeschwader (JG) Fighter wing, includes three or four Gruppen

Jagdwaffe Fighter Arm or Fighter Force

Jagdverband German jet force

Jug Short for Juggernaut, P-47 Thunderbolt

KIA Killed In Action

Kommandeur Commanding officer of a Gruppe

Kommodore Commodore or captain, a Geschwader command position rather than a rank

Liberty Run Night off in town

Little friend USAAF fighter aircraft

LORAN Long-Range Navigation

Lufbery A Lufbery, or "Luftberry," as it was sometimes known in its corrupted form by American fighter pilots, was named for the World War I American fighter ace Major Gervais Raoul Lufbery, who scored seventeen victories. The Lufbery Circle was a defensive tactic, in which a group of aircraft flew in a tight circle, making it difficult for enemy aircraft to break into and attack without themselves being attacked.

Luftwaffe (LW) German Air Force

Milk run An easy mission

MTO Mediterranean Theater of Operations

NAAFI Navy, Army Air Force Institute (British)

NACA National Advisory Committee For Aeronautics

NCO Non-commissioned officer

PFC Poor [expletive] civilian, or private first class

Piccadilly Commando A London prostitute

PoW Prisoner of War

PR Photographic reconnaissance

Purple Heart Medal awarded for wounds recieved in combat

PX Post Exchange (US)

R&R Rest & Recreation

R/T Radio telephony

RCAF Royal Canadian Air Force (now CAF – Canadian Armed Forces)

RCM Radio countermeasures

Reichsverteidigung Air Defense of Germany

RP Rocket projectile

Sack Bed

Schwarm Flight of four aircraft

Schwarmführer Flight leader

Schwarzemänner Ground crews or "black men," so-called because of the color of their tunics

Stab Staff flight

Staffel Roughly equivalent to a squadron, designated sequentially within the Geschwader by Arabic figures, e.g.: 4./JG 1

Staffelkapitän (Stk) Captain, a Staffel command position rather than a rank

TAC Tactical Air Command

UHF Ultra-High Frequency

USAAC United States Army Air Corps

USAAF United States Army Air Force

USSTAF United States Strategic Air Forces (8th and 15th AFs)

VHF Very High Frequency

WAAF (British) Women's Auxiliary Air Force

WREN (British) Women's Royal Navy

Zerstörer "Destroyer," Bf 110 fighter aircraft

Zerstörergeschwader (ZG) Heavy fighter wing (Bf 110 or Me 410 twin-engined fighter)

ZOI Zone of the Interior (USA)

Acknowledgments and Picture Credits

Author acknowledgments

Mike Bailey; Bill Espie; Steve Gotts; Clarence "Buck" G. and Margory "Marge" Haynes; Andy Height; Walt Konantz; Huie Lamb USAF Retd; Nigel McTeer; Ian McLachlan; Larry Nelson, USAF Retd; Lieutenant Colonel Ernie Russell USAF Retd; Peter C. Smith; Bill Smith and Denise Davies of the East Essex Aviation Society Museum; Paul Wilson, and the wonderful staff of the US 2nd Air Division Memorial Library in Norwich.

Editors' acknowledgements

The editors would like to thank the following people for their kind help and advice during the production of this book: Patrick Bunce, Bernard Zee, Jerry Whiting, John Bybee, Dave Donald, Daniel Haulman, and Tom Lauria.

Museums

A large number of the items of memorabilia photographed for this book came from the East Essex Aviation Society Museum. Details of the museum, including location, can be found at: http://www.eastessexaviationsociety.org

Picture credits

Page number and position are indicated as follows: L = Left, TL = top left, TR = top right; C = center; CL = Center left; B = Bottom, etc:

Author's collection: 12–13; 14: C; 15: TL, TR, C; 16: TL, CR; 17: TL, CR; 18: CL; 19: TL, BR; 20: TL, TR, C; 21: CR; 22: C; 23: CL, TR; 24: TC, CR; 25: TR; 26: C; 28: TL, BL; 30: TC, BC; 31: TL, TR, BC; 33: TR, BR; 34: TC, BL; 35: BC; 36–37; 38: C; 39: TC, CL, CR; 41: C, CR; 42: CL, TR; 43: CL; 44–45; 46: BL; 47: TC, BC; 48: TR; 49: TC, CR, CL; 50: CR, BL; 51: CR; 52: BR; 53: TL, BR; 54: TR, BL; 55: TC, CR; 56–57; 58: CR; 59: TL, BL; 60: BR; 61: CR; 62; BL, TR; 63: CR, BC; 64: BR, CL; 65: TL, BR; 66: BC; 67: TC, CR; 68–69; 70: TR, BC; 71: CR; 72: TR, C; 73: CR; 74: TR, BL; 75: BR; 76: BR; 77: BL, BR; 78: BL, BR; 79: C, TR; 80–81; 82: CL, TR; 83: TC, BR; 84: TR, BC, BR; 85: CR; 86: TC, B; 87: CR; 88: BL; 89: BL, CR; 90: BC, CR; 91: B; 92–93; 94: TC, BR; 95: TR, CR; 96: B; 97: BL; 98: TR, BL; 99: BR, BR; 100: CL, BR; 101: TL, BR; 102: BL; 103: TL; 112: C, BL; 113: TR; 116–117; 118: BR; 119: CL, BR; 120: TR x2, CL, CR; 121: TC, CL; 122: TR, CR; 123: TC, TR, BL; 124: CR, BL; 125: TR, B; 126: CL, CR; 128–129; 130: CR; 131: TC; 132: BR; 133: C, CR; 134: CL, B; 136: C, CR; 137: C, BL; 138: TC, BL; 139: TL, BR; 140–141; 142: C; 143: CL; 144: CL; 145: BC, BR; 146: C; 147: TR, BR; 148: TC, CR, BL; 149: TC, TR, C, BL; 150: CL; 151: TC, CL; 152: TR, C; 153: TC, CL

NARA: 18: TR

Alamy: 26: TL

DerHossMeister: 26: TR

Bernard Zee: 27: TR

Radiofan: 27: BR

Patrick Bunce: 28: BR; 29; 32: TL, TR, B; 35: TC

USGOV-PD: 46: TC; 78: TC; 106: C

Kogo: 77: TL

USAF: 104–105; 107: TC, CR; 108: TC, BR; 109: TL, BC; 110: BL, BR; 111: TR; 114: C, BR; 115: TR, C, BR

Jwissik: 107: TL

HMSO: 113: B

MKFI: 119: TL

High Contrast: 135: TL, BR

All the memorabilia and artifact photos featured in this book, with the exception of any listed above, were made by Mark WinWood and are copyright of Elephant Book Company Ltd.

Jacket and front cover illustration:

Roy Grinnell, Artist of the Aces

Website: www.roygrinnell.com